The First Americans

▼ ・ ▼ ・ ▼ ・ ▼ ・ ▼ ・ ▼ ・ ▼ ・ ▼ ・ ▼

INDIANS OF THE PACIFIC NORTHWEST

Karen Liptak

Facts On File
New York • Oxford

About *The First Americans* Series:

This eight-volume series presents the rich and varied cultures of the many Native American tribes, placing each within its geographical and historical context. Each volume covers a different cultural area, providing an understanding of all the major North American Indian tribes in a systematic, region-by-region survey. The series emphasizes the contributions of Native Americans to American culture, illustrating their legacy in striking photographs within the text and in all-color photo essays.

Indians of the Pacific Northwest

Facts On File, Inc.
460 Park Avenue South
New York NY 10016
USA

Facts On File Limited
Collins Street
Oxford OX4 1XJ
United Kingdom

Library of Congress Cataloging-in-Publication Data

Liptak, Karen
    Indians of the Pacific Northwest / Karen Liptak
        p.   cm. — The First Americans series
    Includes index.
    Summary: Examines the history, culture, changing fortunes, and current situation of the various Indian peoples of the Pacific Northwest.
    ISBN 0-8160-2384-0
    1. Indians of North America—Norhwest, Pacific—Juvenile literature.
[1. Indians of North America—Southwest, Pacific.]
    I. Title   II. Series.
    E78.N77L55   1991
    979.5'00497—dc20   90–45547

A British CIP catalogue record for this book is available from the British Library.

Facts On File books are available at special discounts when purchased in bulk quantities for businesses, associations, institutions or sales promotions. Please call our Special Sales Department in New York at 212/683-2244 (dial 800/322-8755 except in NY, AK or HI) or in Oxford at 865/728399.

Design by Carmela Pereira
Jacket design by Donna Sinisgalli
Typography & composition by Tony Meisel

10 9 8 7 6 5 4 3 2 1

This book is printed on acid-free paper.
Manufactured in MEXICO.

▲ A Haida village in Alaska, around 1900.

CONTENTS

▼ • ▼ • ▼ • ▼ • ▼ • ▼ • ▼ • ▼ • ▼

THE PACIFIC NORTHWEST CULTURE AREA

The approximate tribal boundaries of the Pacific Northwest culture area are shown in the larger map, with modern state boundaries. The smaller map shows the culture area in relation to all of North America.

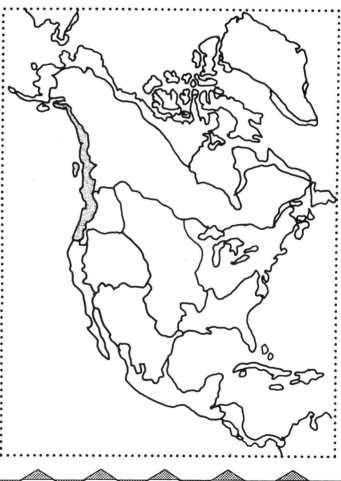

TLINGIT

TONGASS

NISKA

TSIMSHIAN

GITKSAN

HAIDA

HAISLA

BELLA BELLA

BELLA COOLA

HEILTSUK

KWAKIUTL

COMOX

SEECHELT

NOOTKA

PUNTLATCH

SQUAMISH

NANAIMO

SEMIAHMOO

COWICHAN

LUMNI

MAKAH

NOOKSACK

QUILEUTE

SKAGIT

QUINAULT

CLALLAM

SKOKOMISH

HUMPTULIPS

COAST SALISH

CHEHALIS

TWANA

DUWAMISH

CHINOOK

SNOQUALMIE

KWALHIOQUA

CLATSOP

PUYALLUP

CLATSKANIE

NISQALLY

TILLAMOOK

COWLIZ

SILETZ

YAQUINA

ALSEA

KALAPUYA

SUISLAW

COOS

UMPQUA

TUTUTNI

TAKELMA

CHASTACOSTA

0 200 MILES

▲ Native Americans in the village of Klinkwan, Alaska, at the turn of the century.

CHAPTER ONE

ROOTS

he Pacific Northwest Coast Indians lived in a rugged, windswept region, where ocean waves crash against the rocks of steep mountains that seem to rise straight up from the sea. Some mountains end in peaks as high as 4,000 feet tall. The area is located on a narrow strip of land (and nearby islands) of North America's Pacific coast, from Yakutat Bay in southeast Alaska through British Columbia to the mouth of the Columbia River in Washington State.

The mountains extend inland for about a hundred miles, making passage impossible except along trails cut by the major rivers, notably the Nass and Skeena in the north, and the Columbia in the south. The mountains of the Coastal Range cut off the region from the interior.

While the terrain is inhospitable in many places, the climate here is often mild. Constant fogs, rainfall, and moist winds make this a damp region, supportive of lush evergreen forests with abundant vegetation and numerous game animals. The huge trees provided the Pacific Northwest Coast Indians with material for everything from transportation and clothing to homes, cooking tools, and ceremonial headdresses. Many land plants could be gathered and land animals could be hunted for immediate use as well as for food and other needs later on.

But, most importantly, this area abounded in well-stocked waterways. The rivers and streams, as well as the sea, teemed with fish. It was to this natural resource that the coastal people most owed their privileged existence.

But where did these people come from? The Pacific Northwest Coast Indians are believed to have descended from people who originally lived in what is today Mongolia and Siberia. These early inhabitants of North America traveled across a temporary land bridge we today call Beringia. Beringia existed when ice tied up much of the Earth's water during an Ice Age about 10,000 years ago. Scientists debate when human beings first crossed Beringia, but from the dating of ancient articles they have found, they believe that by 9,000 years ago the ancestors of some Pacific Northwest Coast groups had arrived. Other ancestors may have come in subsequent waves of migrations. These newcomers eventually settled in choice locations, wherever they could find shelter and fresh water along the mainland shores, streams, estuaries, and rivers as well as the islands of the new land.

The Pacific Northwest Coast Indians lived in areas that eventually became the Canadian Province of British Columbia, as well as the

▲ This Tlingit woman has a decorative disk, called a labret, through her lower lip.

states of Alaska, Washington, and Oregon. Some of their descendants still live in these places today. The Indians who inhabited this land, while they were divided into separate groups by geography and language, shared a common culture.

THE MAIN GROUPS

The most northerly group was the Tlingit (too-LING-it). They lived in craggy lands along the coast of what is today southeastern Alaska. Their area is known as the Alaskan Panhandle, since on a map it resembles the handle of a cooking pan. The Tlingit also inhabited many of the area's offshore islands. They were to become as well known for their confrontations with the Russian settlers as for their well-crafted canoes and the exquisite blankets made by the Chilkat, one of their tribes.

The Tlingit, along with other more northern tribes, made war on occasion, as did the Nootka and Kwakiutl. However, war did not necessarily involve physical violence. Some battles were carried on through oratory. Groups were known to fight wars with property for status, rather than with weapons.

To the south of the Tlingit lived the Tsimshian (chim-SHEE-an). They made their home on offshore islands and along the coastline as well as the Nass and Skeena rivers in what is today northwestern British Columbia. From the rivers they caught the valuable eulachon, a fish whose oil was widely used by all the coastal Indians. The life-style of the Tsimshian was very similar to that of people who lived directly on the coast and with whom they traded for products that came from the sea.

Some 50 miles off the mainland from the Tsimshian are a cluster of islands known today as the Queen Charlotte Islands; they are now part of British Columbia. Here lived the Haida (HI-duh), builders of the biggest canoes on the coast. The Haida also occupied the islands called Prince of Wales, which today belong to Alaska.

Although the Haida language was related to that of the Tlingit, they formed a distinct group with a reputation for engaging in long and dangerous sea voyages. However, the Haida, Tsimshian, and Tlingit believe that they share a common heritage, and for this reason they held many ceremonies together.

Further south, Bella Coola (bell-UH-kooluh) territory was located on both sides of the icy blue Bella Coola River, which rushes down from the Canadian Rockies into the Pacific Ocean. The Bella Coola were migrants from further south who became much like the tribes they settled near. In time, although their language was different, their life-style became almost identical to that of their close neighbors, the Kwakiutl (kuack-EE-oodle).

The Kwakiutl were best known for the spectacular dances and elaborate feasts they held. They were divided into a northern group and a southern group. The northern group lived on the mainland, while the southern group lived on the north end of Vancouver Island. The Kwakiutl also lived on the bays and inlets around Queen Charlotte Sound.

Vancouver, the largest island (250 miles long) in the region, was also home to the Nootka (NOOT-kaw), who were the coast's greatest whale hunters. The Nootka also lived in Cape Flattery, Washington. They were the first Pacific Northwest Coast natives that European explorers met and lived among. Their language was distantly related to Kwakiutl, and their basic canoe-style was widely imitated throughout the region.

A third group shared Vancouver Island. These were Indians of the Coast Salish (SAY-lish), who lived along the island's southeastern shoreline.

Other Coast Salish tribes lived on the mainland, in southern British Columbia and in most of western Washington State. Their many relatives living along Puget Sound differed in life-style from the Salish groups who lived on the coast. Salish groups also lived in what is today Idaho and Montana.

Across the Straits of Juan Perez from Vancouver Island is the Olympic Peninsula, now a part of Washington State. Here lived the Makah, who were whalers like their close relatives, the Nootka.

Near the Makah in Salish territory lived two smaller whaling groups, the Quileute (Quill-EE-yoot), who were their enemies, and the Quinault (QUINN-alt).

Further south along the Pacific coast lived Indians who shared similar characteristics to their northern neighbors but did everything on a smaller scale. Their homes were not as big, nor were their feasts as lavish. However, one group to note was the Chinook, who lived along the Columbia River and were the greatest traders of the region. They played an important role in intertribal communication, taking goods from coastal Indians to inland Indians and bringing inland goods back to coastal Indians in return.

▲ A Tlingit women with a pin in her lower lip, a form of decoration that replaced the labret as a way to denote status.

INDIAN LANGUAGES

These are the language groups along the Pacific Northwest Coast:

TRIBE	LANGUAGE
Tlingit	Na-Dene
Haida	
Eyak	
Tsimshian	Penutian
Chinook	
Coos	
Alsea	
Siuslaw	
Kalapuya	
Coast Salish	Salishan
Bella Coola	
Chehalis	
Clallam	
Lumni	
Quinault	
Tillamook	
Comox	
Bella Bella	Wakashan
Kwakiutl	
Nootka	
Makah	
Haisla	
Heiltsuk	
Chimakum	Chimakum
Quileute	

▲ Two Nootka men in a dugout canoe. The carved spray shield in front keeps water out of the canoe and off the men.

COASTAL TRAVELS

Although coastal Indians had little more than limited contact with Indians of the interior, they frequently canoed along the coast and the rivers. Social visits were possible since the region's abundant resources gave people much free time to enjoy. Wars were another reason for such voyages. And a brisk trade existed among the coastal tribes long before European traders arrived on the scene.

The people exchanged any excess items that they gathered, hunted, and fished, as well as objects they crafted. They also exchanged ideas, which helped promote a similar culture up and down the coast.

▲ Chilkat children pose in front of a chief's large plank house in Chilkat, Alaska; this photo was taken in 1895.

▲ Two Tlingit girls near Cooper River, Alaska, in 1903.
Their jewelry includes nose rings, which were commonly
worn by both sexes.

▲ Totem poles at the Haida village of Skidegate on the
Queen Charlotte Islands, British Columbia, in a photo
taken around 1910.

▲ The Native Americans of the Pacific Northwest traveled widely up and down their long coastline. Large canoes that could hold a dozen or more people made the journey easy.

▼ The Native Americans of the Pacific Northwest were highly skilled in the art of making canoes. A canoe this large would be used for trading goods up and down the coastline. It could also be used to carry a raiding party.

THE LAND AND ITS PEOPLE

◀ Dancers in traditional costumes pose before a painted house front in Alaska.

▼ Lush forest along the trail to Sunrise Lakes in Mt. Ranier National Park, near Seattle, Washington.

◀ ▲ A land of natural beauty and mystery is revealed by these moss-laden trees and cascading waterfalls in the rain forests of Olympic National Park, western Washington. Here, rainfall averages 150 inches each year.

THE IMPORTANCE OF WOOD

▲ This elaborately painted Haida housefront can be seen today in Sitka, Alaska.

◀ A carved and painted totem pole appears to reach to the sky at the Provincial Museum in Victoria, British Columbia. A painted plank house is behind it.

LIVING ALONG THE PACIFIC COAST

▲ Fog and mist often loom over the forest islands of British Columbia. The region gets a lot of rain but has mild winters.

▶ The Pacific Ocean once bustled with Native American canoe traffic up and down the rocky, misty coast.

▼ The Native Americans of the Pacific Northwest inhabited a narrow strip of land between the Pacific Ocean and the rugged Coast Range. Mountains such as these were always visible.

▲ At 14,410 feet above sea level, Mt. Rainier in Washington is visible on a clear day for nearly a hundred miles in all directions.

CHAPTER TWO

LIVING

n general, the Indians of the Pacific Northwest Coast were the wealthiest, most status-conscious tribes in all of North America. Many of the tribes were deeply concerned with social rank and personal possessions. Before the non-Indian traders, explorers, and settlers came, they lived a unique and somewhat charmed existence for many hundreds of years. While many groups among them appear to have been warlike, their high level of artistry—especially in wood crafting—reveals them to be a creative, ingenious people as well.

Here, too, were people heavily steeped in ritual and tradition. Many Pacific Coast Indians believe that their ancestors were created in the region they now occupy. In the rush of Europeans, Russians, and Americans to acquire the riches of the Pacific Northwest Coast for themselves in the 18th and 19th centuries, the native culture of the Pacific Northwest Indians was very nearly destroyed.

Within 150 years of the newcomers' arrival in the mid-1700s, the number of Pacific Northwest Coast Indians plummeted. Much of the destruction was intentional, as the Indians were forced to assimilate or chased off their lands. In other cases, the destruction was unintentional, as when diseases brought by the Europeans reached epidemic proportions among the Indians.

However, the story of the Pacific Northwest Coast Indians is not over yet. Today, the descendants of these proud and gifted people are experiencing a revival of their traditions. Equally significant, appreciation for their works of art and ceremonial creations is growing among Indians and non-Indians alike.

VILLAGE LIFE

Most Indians on the coast lived in two villages, a summer one and a winter one. They set up simple brush shelters or wooden structures in their summer villages, which were usually erected along rivers, where the food was plentiful. Here, the people caught their salmon and dried them in rows in the summer sun. The winter villages had more substantial wooden homes. These villages were situated in sheltered sites within easy reach of the beaches. They consisted of a single line of cedar wood houses with their entrances facing the coast. Visitors arriving in the area by sea were greeted by lines of totem poles. Most people have probably seen pictures of these intricately carved wooden poles. Some groups had free-standing totem poles in front of the houses. Others had poles that served as house posts;

▲ A group of Chinook relax inside their lodge while dinner is cooking. Dried fish hang from rafters in this 1839 engraving.

these supported the heavy logs that formed the main roof beams.

A village could have 30 or more houses with anywhere from a dozen to a hundred people living in a single multi-family dwelling. The Coast Salish groups called these massive structures "long houses." All the other coastal tribes called them "big houses." Over a thousand people could inhabit a single coastal village.

Each village had a leading house that served a dual purpose; it was lived in and also used for holding ceremonies. The leading houses were often painted with symbols from the house chief's ancestry.

No other North American Indians valued rank and wealth as much as those on the Pacific Northwest Coast. The family into which you were born greatly influenced your rights and privileges from birth to death.

Families were related according to their kinship ties. In the north, such ties were based on the mother's side of the family. A child received his or her place in the community from the mother's ancestry.

Further south, such rights were generally based on the father's side. Among the Kwakiutl who lived in the central area, children were heirs to the heritage of both their parents.

This was also true for Coast Salish groups, where children inherited rank and responsibilities from both sides of the family.

The basic family unit was the household, which consisted of either clan or blood relations, depending upon the group. Clans are social divisions, which go back to legendary beginnings. Each clan and each household had an ancient history and many traditions that were passed on in stories told by the elders. These stories united the people in each clan.

The clans had crests, sometimes known as totems, which adorned many objects, especially totem poles. A crest is a representation of animals or supernatural beings believed to have assisted ancestors of that social division, or clan.

The Tlingit had two large clans, called Raven and Wolf. The Haida also had two major clans, Eagle and Raven. Among the Tsimshian were Raven, Eagle, Wolf, and Whale. These clans were subdivided into smaller ones. The Tlingit, Tsimshian, and Haida all believed that their clans and sub-clan divisions were related. This led to these three northernmost groups participating in many ceremonies together.

▲ The interior of a Northwest Indian home in Alaska, as drawn by a member of Captain Cook's crew in the late 1700s.

All clan members, regardless of their tribe of origin, are considered relatives and marriage between them is forbidden. Therefore, if a Haida husband was a Raven, he could never marry a woman from the Raven clan. Instead, his wife had to come from the Eagle clan. The couple's sons and daughters would be brought up as Eagles, since a Haida man's children belong to his wife's clan.

Among the Tlingit, Tsimshian, and Haida, a man's heir was not his own son, but rather his sister's son, his nephew. In order for the boy to learn about the special rights and responsibilities he would inherit someday, he had to leave his parents' household while he was still a young child and go to live with his uncle's family.

Most of the northernmost groups organized clans into two larger groupings, known as moieties or halves. Membership in a moiety was based on the mother, and each member had to marry someone from the opposite moiety. This meant that a man and his children were always in opposite moieties.

Most of the Pacific Northwest Coast tribes had four main divisions or classes in each village. The villages were each economically independent, with a head chief whose inherited position made him the highest-ranking member of the most important family there. He also was usually the wealthiest man in the community, for he was expected to hold many feasts and help the poor, old, and orphaned. Each clan also had a chief; so did each household. The relatives of the various chiefs formed a kind of superior class. In some groups, members who possessed valued skills, like totem pole carving or whaling, also formed a special class. The others in the village were all commoners, except for two more classes: shamans and slaves.

The shamans were doctors. When the people became ill, they turned to the shamans to cure them with rituals, medicines, and special powers. The people also counted on the shamans to help them receive good fortune in their every endeavor and throughout life.

Slavery was a way of life in this region, especially among the Haida and the Tlingit. Slaves never came from the same tribe that held them. Rather, they were captured in raiding parties to other groups. A family's status increased as it acquired more slaves.

Slaves were generally not considered part of their owner's family, although there are some stories of slaves who became very well loved. Slaves were only allowed to marry other slaves. Any sons and daughters they had became slaves, too. Slaves could be sold, as well as traded and given away.

Occasionally, slaves were badly treated, or even killed as a way of showing wealth. By killing a slave, the owner was implying, "I'm so wealthy, I don't even need that slave." Such killings were done according to ritual and with special weapons.

RITUAL AND TRADITION

From birth, every passage of life for Indians of the Northwest was marked by ritual and tradition. Women had their babies in a separate house, away from everyone else. Babies wore diapers made of moss that were wrapped in animal skins. They were tied to cradleboards, which mothers either carried or hung from a roof beam. Babies were named after an ancestor. Later in life, a child could get another name from the father's side of the family at a huge feast known as a potlatch.

When an Indian boy on the Pacific Northwest Coast reached the age of manhood, usually at 12 or 13 years old, he was expected to seek his Guardian Spirit. These spirits dominated the life of the coastal people, and they primarily took the form of the familiar animals the people often saw. Once a boy found his personal Guardian Spirit, it would assist him throughout his life. A youngster's Guardian Spirit invisibly entered his soul and taught him many things, both practical and ceremonial. For instance, a fisherman's Guardian Spirit teaches him how to use a spear as well as to perform special songs and dances.

But first the spirit had to be found. It was feared that girls might get kidnapped if they wandered away alone, so they were only allowed to receive their Guardian Spirit if it came to them while they were going about their daily chores. However, a boy found his Guardian Spirit through a special ritual that all boys were expected to observe.

The time to seek a boy's spirit was in the winter. During this season of short days, a boy had to first take a purifying bath in an icy stream. Then he had to leave his village and go off alone

▲ This elaborately carved seat was made for a Haida chief. The carving on the backrest represents a halibut.

into the woods. He was expected to stay there, wandering around, and waiting for his spirit to come. Although he could make a fire to stay warm, he was not supposed to eat. A boy would be considered a failure if no spirit ever came to him. However, one usually did.

Future canoe makers often had woodpeckers as their Guardian Spirits, and fishermen had salmon and cod, as well as birds that ate fish. Warriors had hornets as Guardian Spirits, and hunters had wolves. This would be the start of a lifelong relationship. As the boy grew into a man, and then became an elder, his Guardian Spirit would stay with him, to grant him additional skills as well as personal traits, such as courage.

Whether or not a girl received a Guardian Spirit, she went through a special ritual when she reached child-bearing age. In many villages, she was confined to a dark, hideaway for a few weeks. There she was under the care of her grandmother, who made sure that the girl's movements and diet were carefully restricted.

Girls approaching puberty had to fast for a certain number of days. They also had food taboos, some of which would last for years. These included a ban on eating fresh salmon, the main food along the coast.

A young woman was considered very powerful at this time. Her very look could be threatening. Therefore, when she left her retreat during this period she wore a hood on her head so she didn't harm people, hunting and fishing equipment, or nature.

At this same time, when a girl was generally in her early teens, those from the wealthier Tlingit, Tsimshian, and Haida families received their first labret. This was a lip ornament that told everyone that the wearer had become of marriageable age.

In this region, marriage was regarded as a social contract between a husband and wife as well as between their respective families. The higher their rank, the more restricted Pacific Northwest Coast Indians were in their marriage choices.

Among the northern groups, marriage was forbidden within one's own clan. A Tsimshian man, like a Haida and Tlingit man, was expected to marry a woman from his father's clan. But other restrictions also applied.

For instance, a Tsimshian man frequently married his mother's younger brother's daughter. Two of the most important Tsimshian tribes had a custom for the head chiefs to wed each other's sisters. The complicated choices led to inequalities of age. In the north, when a man died, his sister's son was expected to inherit his property as well as to marry the deceased chief's widow.

Among the Bella Coola intermarriage was customary between certain families in order to keep social possessions and position within a confined circle. A father might have his daughter marry several men, one after the other, even before she reached womanhood. In this way he was assured that his grandchildren would receive their mother's acquired honors, regardless of who each one's father was.

Each family sought a marriage match that raised its social status in the community. Generally, the groom's family started the marriage formalities by speaking about it with the girl's family. Then they held a feast at which they praised the boy's virtues. They gave many speeches, related their family histories, and presented the bride's kin with gifts. The gifts were known as the bride-price. The higher the rank of the couple, the greater the bride-price was.

Among the Nootka it was customary to refuse the bride-price at least three times. The gifts had to be carried to the girl's house, then back to the boy's house again and again before they could be accepted. The higher the girl's social position, the more refusals her family made. By their refusals the girl's family was saying that her great virtues were deserving of a very special mate.

All the groups except the Tlingit expected that once a bride-price was accepted, it would be repaid. Exchanges between the families continued throughout the couple's married life. These were made at major ceremonies. To keep in the good graces of the other side's kin, it was important that repayments were on time and sufficient.

When a Kwakiutl bride and groom married, the bride's father announced that his son-in-law would receive certain property, honors, and names. These were usually not due until the bride gave birth to a child, or until the child was old enough to be initiated into the ceremonies. The payment ended the marriage. The wife was now free to stay with her husband or return to her parents' house. The husband could renew his marriage by giving gifts to his father-in-law. Eventually, these would be repaid in new honors, property, and names he received.

Some chiefs had more than one wife. This was a way to show off their wealth. Among the Tlingit, where women held major positions in the tribal hierarchy, a wife sometimes took several husbands.

Although getting married involved much ritual, getting divorced was simple. It required one party to move to another residence. However, such actions could sometimes result in insult and disgrace, which were major concerns to the people of this region. Basically, an insult meant any damaging statement, even if it was a true one. Sometimes insults could be resolved by paying a fine. Other times, insults could result in armed feuds that could go on for years.

The general belief about death was that the dead went to a better place. However, it was a lonely place, and the dead often wanted to return to take some of the living with them for company. The danger of being snatched by the dead was greatest for the deceased's relatives. Therefore, they generally left funeral rituals to those outside the family. Often these funeral bearers were repaid with ceremonies, such as a potlatch.

Burial customs varied along the Pacific Northwest Coast. The Tsimshian cremated, or burned, the dead after removing the heart, which they buried in the earth. The Haida and Tlingit also burned their dead. However, these three groups had special procedures for their shamans, or medicine people. The Tsimshian burned the shaman's internal organs before burying them in an above-ground grave house. Haida and Tlingit gathered a shaman's bones after cremation and put them in boxes above the ground. Tree burial was common among the Nootka and the southern Kwakiutl. They folded up the bodies of the deceased and put them inside big wooden boxes that were placed high upon a tree some distance from the village. Among the Nootka, the highest-ranking families also had burial caves. The Sa-

lish hung their dead in trees, but the bodies were placed in canoes rather than in boxes.

All the tribes erected monuments near the burial places of their most prestigious people. These were usually wooden carvings with the main crests of the dead person. Among the Tlingit, memorials for the dead were the main occasions for potlatches. Burial was by the opposite clan, and they received the gifts at the potlatch.

CEDAR FORESTS

The tall cedar trees that grow in the lush forests of the Pacific Northwest Coast were as important to the native peoples here as were their plentiful fish. Cedar provided the Indians with material for their homes, transportation, clothing, cooking utensils, tools, and baskets, ceremonial headdresses, boxes, and implements.

Red cedar was found in the south and yellow cedar grew in the north. In both sections, cedar was highly valued since it is so straight-grained and water-resistant. The latter was an excellent quality to have in this rain-soaked area, where the people spent much time outdoors and in water-going vessels. They made their canoes out of cedar.

Many blankets were made from shredded cedar, or a combination of cedar and mountain goat hair. Mats were woven from cedar, too. And the famous Pacific Northwest Coast totem poles, which we will discuss later on, were skillfully carved from cedar wood.

The great cedar trees were felled with tools known as adzes, made out of elk horn or nephrite, which is a kind of jade. These are chopping tools that resemble a hatchet. Controlled burning was often used at the tree base.

When a tree was made into boards or planks for the covering of Northwest Coast homes, these were often split directly out of a living tree. This was done by pounding in wedges with a tough stone hand maul (hammer) and then pulling the plank away from the tree. Then the wood could be shaped into huge beams and posts with an adze and chisel blades. Boards were also split from trees already on the ground as a result of storms. Red cedar was the best wood in the region for planks since it was easiest to split.

When wood needed to be smoothed, abrasives were used, such as slabs of sandstone, sharkskin, and grit. It also appears that among their tools, the people here had iron knives long before they established trade relations with the Europeans.

Where did the metal come from? One suggestion is that it was found in wrecked ships. Another possibility is that the Indians traded with tribes from Siberia, where iron was mined.

HOMES AND CLOTHING

Homes along the Pacific Northwest Coast were commonly made out of cedar planks. A feature common to the houses of all tribes in the area is an independent inner main framework and an outside covering or shell. The inner framework lasted from year to year, while the outside shell might be removed and taken to a new location or permanently destroyed after the death of the house chief.

However, there were stylistic differences in northern, central, and southern areas. The homes in the north were usually more massive and square-shaped than those in the south. While the Tlingit and the Haida had similar homes, the Haida were the best woodworkers of the coast. Their houses could be 60 feet in width as well as in length. The homes had four corner posts, two end posts, and additional side posts. The front pole post loomed above the roof. It was carved and painted with family crests. An opening in this post served as the elegant entrance to a Haida home.

Northern roofs were gabled, similar to Nootka, Bella Coola, and Kwakiutl homes, with a hole left for smoke to get out at the ridge. There were no windows in these homes. Therefore, sunlight came in only through the smoke hole and the doorway. Many families lived in each of these shelters, but they all shared a common fireplace, contained in a rectangular pit dug in the middle of the house.

Further south, the Kwakiutl and the Nootka homes were large, with gable roofs framed around a central rectangular pit. These people moved their villages more often than their northern neighbors. Each house had many removable planks around its permanent wooden frame. People carried their family's planks with them from one location to another. They entered their houses through a simple opening in front.

Inside these homes, each family had its own fire and let the smoke out by pushing aside a roof plank with a pole. The Nootka carved faces on their house posts, but the meaning of them is not known. Family crests were usually painted on the outside front wall of the house. A carved family crest might also top a tall free-standing

▲ The front of this Kwakiutl plank house is elaborately painted with symbols representing eagles and killer whales.

pole near the doorway.

The Salish homes were much longer than any others built in the north. In fact, these undecorated houses were practically villages in themselves, some as long as 1,500 feet. They were built with a sloped roof, with the higher long side facing the beach.

Although interior details differed among various peoples in the region, families were always assigned spaces according to social rank. The most important family was always farthest from the entrance.

The most frequently found items of furniture in the house were handsomely carved cedar chests. Possessions, as well as dried foods, were stored in these chests. In some cases, the chests also served as partitions between family spaces.

Cedar mats were used to separate sections of the house, too. In the leading homes, the partitions were removed for ceremonies, to make room for audiences and performers.

The men, women, and children in this region usually wore as little clothing as possible. Most of what they did wear was made out of cedar bark. Sea otter skins and mountain goat wool were two other materials from which clothes were made.

Throughout most of the year, Indian men went naked. When they did get dressed, their main item of clothing was a blanket woven out of cedar bark. The Indian women usually wore skirts made from shredded cedar bark or grass that was hung over a waist cord. This looked like a Polynesian "hula skirt." Another cedar bark garment covered them from shoulders to ankles.

Basketlike hats were worn as protection against the rain, as well as the sun. Some of these hats were the prize possessions of village chiefs.

They were most often woven of spruce roots. Tlingit men and women trimmed some of their hats with sea otter fur. The Tsimshian wore tall, pointed hats woven of cedar bark and grass. Among the Nootka, the hats worn by chiefs were distinguished by pointed knobs on the top. These were often decorated with events, such as whale hunting. Haida hats, which were flatter, had crest animals painted on them.

During the area's frequent rains, both sexes wore ponchos of shredded cedar to keep dry. These garments could be double-woven to make them warmer. When it was cold the Kwakiutl wore skin shirts and wool capes woven from mountain goat or dog hair. (The Salish raised white dogs that they sheared for wool.)

Except in the far north of the region, men and women went barefoot throughout the year. The northernmost groups sometimes wore buckskin trousers and moccasins that were made in one piece, like a child's pajamas.

Yarn was sometimes needed for making clothes, and cedar bark was the main source for it. The bark was soaked in water for at least two weeks, then beaten with clubs to get rid of the woody parts. A wooden blade was used to shred the fiber against the edge of a plank. A coarse yarn was formed, which could then be bleached and dyed. The long fiber strands were often twisted into yarn by rolling them against the thigh. However, this was also done by the Kwakiutl and other groups with the use of a spindle.

On ceremonial occasions men wrapped a rectangular robe around their bodies. This was often made out of sea otter skins or woven fiber. Chilkat robes were also reserved for ceremonial wear. The woolen robes woven by the Chilkat, a division of the Tlingit, are regarded as among the world's finest. The wool came from mountain goats, or from the small white dogs that the Indians of Puget Sound raised and sheared. The wool could be dyed before being woven so that blues, blacks, and yellows were possible colors. It was then combined with cedar bark fiber.

The Chilkat robes were used as shawls and dancing costumes. As we will discover later on, the blankets also served as a form of exchange, like money.

At ceremonies, the rich could wear their robes with knee-high leggings, special tunics, and aprons. These were worn with wooden headdresses that had crowns of sea lion whiskers. Ceremonial costumes were further enhanced by white down strewn over the hair as a symbol of

▲ Two Nootka women, with woven baskets on their backs and cedar bark capes around their shoulders, sit by the shore.

peace, and strips of buckskin and pelts of ermine hanging down from the headdress.

Painted designs, like those found on family crests and totem poles, adorned ceremonial costumes. The Chilkat and Tlingit wove their designs into their woolen garments. When they began trading with Europeans and cloth was available, they often sewed designs cut out of red flannel to their new clothes.

The traditional ceremonial blanket of the Kwakiutl was the button blanket, decorated with shells as well as buttons. After the coming of the European traders, this garment was often made from the British and Canadian Hudson's Bay Company's woolen trade blankets.

Among the more southern groups, flattening a baby's head was a common procedure. A flattened forehead that sloped back from the eyes was considered a sign of wealth. To achieve this effect, a baby born into a rich Coast Salish, Chinook, or Nootka family was strapped to a board. Then a second board, which was padded, was pressed on the forehead. The gradual result was a flattened skull in front. The Kwakiutl used a different method for reshaping heads. They bound both sides of a baby's head, so that it became elongated upward to a point.

Although the more northerly nations did not flatten foreheads, they had their own unique way to show prestige. A woman's wealth was measured by the size of the lip plug she wore. This plug, known as a labret, was an oval disk that was worn in a slit pierced into a woman's lower lip. Labrets were most often made out of wood or bone. The time for a woman's first labret was when she reached puberty. The slit was enlarged and a larger labret added as women got older.

While only women of the northern tribes wore labrets, both sexes all along the coast wore nose and ear ornaments. These were made from many natural materials, such as bone, copper, fur, and wood. Spiral shells were especially desirable nose decorations since they were rare and only available to the more wealthy. The number of ornaments a person could wear was generally determined by his or her social rank.

Face and body painting was also common. Paints were made by mixing colored powder with deer or bear fat or whale oil. Red came from red ocher, white came from white clay, and black came from soot from a fire. Early reports from white settlers told of Nootka who painted their faces differently every day. In fact, on some days the Nootka painted their faces one way in the morning and another way in the afternoon.

Tattooing was a widespread custom until the beginning of the 20th century. Tattoos ranged from simple stripes on the face in some areas to the Haida's elaborate crest designs, sometimes covering the entire body. Tattoos were made by piercing holes in the skin with objects such as thorns or bones, and then rubbing in charcoal. The Haida used bear grease as a cosmetic base to which they adhered the materials used in both face and body painting. In many areas, before Indians went visiting or greeted guests, they rubbed their hair with bear grease, then stuck white feathers in it.

FOOD

On the Pacific Northwest Coast the chiefs claimed ownership of the hunting lands. Every year, when the hunting, fishing, or gathering season began, a ritual was performed. The chief called a meeting of his group. He reminded everyone that the hunting area was his. Then he generously offered it to the people to use, his offer reflecting on his greatness. The first animals caught or the first plants gathered went to the chief as a gift. When such gifts were collected,

PROTECTION FROM THE RAIN

A Pacific Northwest Coast Indian woman carefully paints an intricate design on an elegant spruce root hat, which will serve as needed protection against the region's frequent rains. Hats such as this took a long time and a great deal of skill to make.

the chief and his family invited the whole village to a big feast.

Fish were the main food source on the Pacific Northwest Coast. Of all the fish, salmon was the most important.

Each spring and summer, enormous numbers of salmon traveled in from the seas to the rivers and streams where they would breed and then die. This was known as their spawning run. Their young returned to the sea and began the life cycle all over again. Eventually they too would swim upstream just as their parents had done, then breed and die.

A special ritual was performed annually when the salmon returned to the rivers after living in the Pacific for three or more years. During this respectful occasion, the undamaged skeleton of the first salmon caught from each river was thrown back into the waters it had been taken from. This was done in order for the fish to be reborn beneath the sea. It was feared that if any bones were missing, the salmon would be deformed when it came back to life.

In some places, fishermen caught salmon with spears or harpoons (a spear with a detachable head) that they thrust at the salmon when they came to the rapids, heading for the shallow pools above them. The fish could only get past these rapids by hurling themselves into the air.

Salmon and other fish were also trapped with weirs. A weir is a wooden or wicker fence that extends across a river. Fish can't swim around it, nor can they go under it or above it. They wind up huddling together just below the water's surface. By standing on a fishing platform above the weir, a person can spear many fish in a short period of time. Large dipping nets were also used to catch the salmon as they struggled upstream.

When the men returned home with their fish, the women immediately cleaned the catch, so the fish wouldn't spoil. Knives were used to slit the salmon into strips that were hung on racks to be dried in the sun or smoked, then stored for the winter. Salmon eggs were considered a delicacy and these, too, were sun-dried or smoked. Large feasts were usually held to celebrate the end of each spawning run, and fresh salmon steaks were served at these.

Besides the salmon, another important fish for the coastal natives was the eulachon, which also swam upstream to spawn in the spring and summer. This small fish was known by white settlers as the candlefish because when dried it was oily enough to be fitted with a wick and lit like a

▲ A fine example of a button blanket. The maker obtained the blanket from white traders and then decorated it with red cloth, pieces of shell, and buttons. The design represents a killer whale.

candle. Eulachon was most abundant in the Nass River, where the fish first arrived each year in March. The Tsimshians, who lived along this river, caught the eulachon with long, funnel-shaped nets. Then they boiled the pungent-smelling oil out of it.

Eulachon oil was used for seasoning other food, which was either dipped directly into it or into a tasty sauce made from it. Containers of this oil were always served at ceremonial feasts.

Halibut was another valuable food source. These large flat fish were caught in shallow bays along the coast with barbed hooks made from hardwood and bone. (Hooks were useless for catching salmon since they stopped eating when they were on their spawning runs and so would not be lured by hooks and bait.)

Herring, flounder, sardines, and sturgeon were four more fish found here. Herring was caught with a herring rake, which looked like a giant wooden comb. It had razor-sharp prongs made of bone. While one person paddled a canoe, the other dragged the herring rake through the water; the herring were impaled on the prongs. The spawn of herring was also collected for food. This could be done by weighing down cedar or hemlock brush in places where the herring spawned. When the brush was removed from the water, it was covered with herring eggs.

Nets were also used; most commonly these were made from nettle fiber that had been dried and spun with the aid of a spindle. Then the

▲ Indian fishermen on wooden platforms use big dipping nets to catch salmon along the Columbia River in 1899.

strands were made into twine. Nets were also made from spruce root and the inner bark of some trees.

Shellfish were another source of food along the Pacific coast. Harvesting them was often done with no special tools. Mussels, limpets, and oysters could be picked up from the rocks with little trouble. However, a pointed stick known as a digging stick was helpful, especially when digging out clams from mud flats and sandy beaches. Clams were roasted or steam-cooked for immediate use. They were also preserved, by removing the clams from the shells and stringing them on sticks for smoking over a fire.

Coastal Indians hunted the seals, sea lions, and sea otter that often came close to shore in search of the fish they lived upon. These animals were sought for their meat, as well as their fur.

A bull sea lion might weigh as much as 1,500 pounds and feed a whole village for many days. On the other hand, sea otters were mostly hunted for their thick, soft fur. It was the discovery of the huge profits to be made by trading sea otter fur that prompted the first strong interest of Europeans in the Pacific Northwest Coast.

Seal hunters traveled in small, two-person canoes to reach the islands where seals basked on the shore. There, they used harpoons with two points to take their prey. The harpoons had floats made from seal bladder. Seal hunters also carried wooden clubs with which they hit a seal over the head as soon as it was harpooned.

The Kwakiutl sometimes hunted seals during the night of the new moon, when there were phosphorescent plankton (tiny plants and animals) in the water. This kind of plankton lights up the waters and reveals the movement of the seals beneath it.

The whale was an important marine animal to the coastal Indians, but few men actually hunted it, since whaling was both difficult and dangerous. The most famous whalers were the Nootka. The Makah, Quinault, and Quileute also prided themselves on being good whalers. Whaling was highly respected, and the daring men who could capture the whale gained esteem in their villages.

The whaling leader usually had an inherited position and was believed to possess great religious power. Before beginning a hunt, he retreated to a special prayer structure, where many carved wooden figures and the skulls of previous whale leaders surrounded him. There, he performed secret rituals to invoke his Guardian Spirit's help to guarantee the hunt's success.

Among the Makah, leaders sang songs to the whales. These songs, passed down from generation to generation, were meant to convince the whales to appear and provide the people of the tribe with food.

Some whaling leaders dressed for the hunt in uncomfortable outfits made from stinging nettles or thorns from wild rosebushes. This was to prove how tough they were.

Whalers traveled in special whaling canoes hollowed out from the trunks of giant cedar trees. The canoes were about 30 feet in length, and they were carved and painted with animal designs, including whales. They could hold eight men, each of whom had a designated task. A whale hunt called for at least three large canoes. Sometimes the fleet was as large as 10.

The whales were killed with harpoons. The harpoons had tips with broad blades made from shell or stone, and antler barbs lashed to them. The shafts were made from yew wood and the lines were made from whale sinew or tendon. When a whale was struck, the head detached from the harpoon.

Each harpoon had one or more sealskin floats attached to it. Once the whale was harpooned, the floats kept the whale from sinking below the water. They also served as drags so that the whales could be driven closer to the shore before they were killed. This cut down on the amount of towing needed to get them to the local beach.

In order for whalers to thrust the harpoon accurately into the whale, they had to get very close to it. From their canoe they tried to get their harpoon as near as possible to the whale's head, since striking the tail could be disastrous;

one swish of it might overturn the canoe.

Although the Nootka usually killed the whales with harpoons, very daring whalers sometimes jumped on the harpooned whale's back and rode it as they thrust a knife into it. If the hunter could stay on the whale until it went under the water, then resurfaced, he was considered a hero in his village.

Whale flesh as well as whale skin were eaten. The intestines were made into containers for oil, and the sinew was used for making rope. The whaler who threw the first harpoon was rewarded with the best pieces of whale blubber. The rest was split between the people in the community, according to each family's rank.

Land hunting was practiced to a limited extent by most Pacific Northwest tribes, being of most importance in communities that were farthest from the salt water. The most important land mammals were bear, mountain goat, deer, and elk. In the northern region, moose was also of value.

Bear meat was considered very tasty, and bear oil was used for several purposes. In the early summer, coastal natives spread it over their bodies to keep away black flies and mosquitos, and year-round they used bear fat in cooking. The bear's fur also was valuable, and comfortable mattresses could be made from it.

Dances were often performed before a big bear hunt in order to ask the spirit of the bear to provide the hunters with food. During a bear dance, the performers carried artificial bear claws between their fingers. They also stomped and grunted, as if they were bears.

Bears were sometimes hunted with the aid of dogs, which can outrun them. The dogs picked up the scent of a bear. Then the hunters followed the dogs until the bear they were chasing became exhausted. The Indians would also hide near the streams in which bears fished for salmon. When the unsuspecting hungry bear approached, a hunter ambushed it with a bow and arrow.

Mountain goats were not found on the islands. However, among mainland tribes, like the Coastal Salish, they were important land animals. The meat was eaten, blankets were made from the prized goat wool, and food dippers were made from its horns. A Salish goat hunter ceremonially painted his face with symbols he had seen in a dream. This ritual was meant to guarantee the success of the hunt, even if the paint washed off before a goat was caught. Like the bears, goats were also chased with hunting dogs.

▲ A fisherman in a woven cedar bark garment prepares to spear his food from the plentiful Pacific.

Deer were also shot with a bow and arrows, which were carried around in cases known as quivers. While many North American Indians made quivers out of animal fur, the Northwest Coast Indians also used an elongated cedar box.

Like Indians throughout North America, Northwest Coast Indians were careful to say prayers both before and after an animal was caught. They feared that if an animal were insulted or abused, its soul might withdraw the privilege of allowing people to feed upon it in the future.

Many wild plants were used by coastal Indians for food as well as for medicine and for making various products. Among those plants eaten were a variety of wild fruits, including wild strawberries, blackberries, huckleberries, and raspberries. Once gathered, berries were usually dried on mats in the sun and then preserved in oil for year-round eating.

▲ Rows of salmon, the most important food in the area, drying in the sun in an Alaskan coastal village.

▲ Shellfish such as clams and abalone were plentiful. They were easily harvested along the beach, with the use of a stick to dig them up or pry them from rocks.

One of the favorite fruits in this region was wild crabapple, which was served with oil. Soapberries were also popular. These were crushed and then beaten with eulachon oil into a frothy Indian "ice cream." This tasty treat was more bitter than the ice cream popular today. It was eaten with a special paddle-shaped soapberry spoon.

Indians in this region, especially in British Columbia, also ate parts of fern, including bracken, which is abundant in wet forests. The young leaves, known as fiddleheads, are considered the most tasty part of the fern and are usually boiled.

In southern British Columbia and in Washington and Oregon the camass is plentiful. This relative of the lily and onion, with a showy cluster of blue or white flowers in the spring, was the main source of starch in the area. Camass bulbs were harvested in late summer when baskets of them were dried and stored for the winter, at which time they were cooked in underground pit ovens.

While the Indians cultivated few plants before Europeans came, raspberry bushes were sometimes pruned to remove any dead plant matter that could keep new shoots from growing. Tobacco was also cultivated. It could be found in small gardens near the villages. Before the Europeans came, tobacco was not smoked. Instead, it was reduced to a powder in small stone bowls known as mortars and then chewed with lime. The lime was obtained by burning clam shells.

COOKING

Cooking was most commonly achieved by using hot stones. Stones of various sizes were an essential part of a woman's cooking equipment. She chose them for their quality, size, and smoothness. The stones were heated, then quickly picked up with wooden sticks and dipped in a container of water to wash off the ashes. Next, they were transferred to a waterproof wooden box, basket, or hollowed-out log that was partially filled with water. The stones were hot enough to make the water boil. An openwork basket with the raw food was then placed into the water, and additional red-hot stones were packed around it. Fish, vegetables, and meat could be boiled in this way.

Stones were also used in baking. A shallow pit was dug and the bottom filled with large, flat

pebbles. Then a fire was built over the pebble bed. Once the pebbles were heated, the fire was removed from them and the food was placed on top to bake.

Pit cooking was another method used here. This required that a fire be built inside a pit, the food added, and the pit covered so the steam would stay in it.

GAMES

Games were very important to the Pacific Northwest Indians. Children as well as adults enjoyed playing them. In fact, youngsters never stopped playing games; as they got older, they substituted more adult games for those of their childhood. Games provided relaxation and a way to keep fit. For adults, games were also a form of gambling.

Many common materials in the area were used by the adults to make a variety of play items for the young. Nootka Indian women made dolls from shredded cedar bark for their children. The Nootka also made tops out of bone and ivory. But Nootka youngsters could not play with whistles,

▲ Makah Indians strip a whale in Neah Bay, Washington, around 1910. Whales produced a bounty of products, from oil and meat to bone and sinew.

since these were used in many rituals.

One of their games was a kind of tag. It began with the children holding hands in a circle. Then they ran sideways as fast as they could. Finally, with the momentum built up, they all let go. The

▲ Carved wooden armor protected a warrior's neck from spear wounds.

▲ These arrows were used for catching sea otters. The barbed copper points are detachable, but the line keeps them from being lost if the sea otter tries to escape after being shot.

boys and girls who got dizzy enough to fall down became "it." They had to chase the others. Every player who got tagged helped catch the rest. The game didn't end until nobody was left to tag.

Another kind of Nootka tag was played on the beach. A child threw a clam shell as far as possible. The others ran after it. Whoever picked it up first was then chased until he or she threw the shell and the race for it began all over again.

Pacific Northwest Coast children also played "fish trap." In this game, one person was called "the fish," and all the other players were the fishermen. The fish got a short head start. Then the fishermen joined hands to make a net in which to catch the fish.

Laughing competitions were very popular games among Nootka of every age. Men and women generally played as one individual against another, but children played as teams. The object was to stare at another, or at the whole other team, with a stern expression on your face. The first person or side to break down and laugh, or even smile, lost the round.

Sometimes the game was played with two teams. Each team chose a representative. He or she was the challenger. Two challengers faced each other while the rest of their teams tried their best to make the other team's challenger smile or laugh. They might make faces, or silly gestures, or shout funny remarks. Each time a team's challenger broke down a new team member replaced the challenger.

Among the many gambling games that were popular with adults, a favorite was the stick game. It was played with a bundle of sticks ranging in number from 10 to over 100. These often had distinctive carvings or paintings on them. The Haida, Tlingit, and other Northwest Coast Indians had highly polished, exquisitely carved or painted gaming sticks. Some were inlaid with small pieces of ivory or shell. The sets of sticks

were kept in pouches made of leather or skin.

A player divided the bundle in half. The object of the game was to guess which half had a particular marked stick, or whether a division had an odd or even number of sticks in it. The same game could also be played with a bundle of reeds or flat disks.

CANOES

Northwest Coast Indians used canoes for whaling, sealing, and fishing, as well as for general transportation.

Building canoes was hard, time-consuming work. It required skill as well as patience. Every man could make his own small, family canoe for traveling around the shallow waters of the rivers and inlets. Women used these small canoes for fishing or for local visiting. However, it took the greatly respected experts to build the larger ocean-going canoes. These were constructed and used primarily by the Haida, Nootka, and Tlingit.

The Haida built the largest canoes. These were 60 feet or more in length, and held over a dozen men. In such vessels the Haida traveled as far as 800 miles from their homes to visit Puget Sound in the south.

Each canoe was made from a hollowed-out log of a cedar tree. Canoe-makers began by first looking for a fallen cedar tree. These were common, due to the many storms in the region. If no fallen tree was found, one was cut down. The trees nearest the streams were most desirable, since they could be floated down to the village with the minimum of transportation. The tree was stripped of bark and branches and then hollowed out with fire. A stone adze was used to chip away the charred sections.

When the log was properly hollowed, water was poured into it, then heated rocks were added. The hot rocks made the water boil. This, in turn, softened the wood. Now, spreaders made of wooden boards were inserted between the sides of the vessel to widen it. These canoe spreaders, known as thwarts, also served as seats.

A spray shield to keep waves from washing inboard was created by adding a piece of carved

cedar wood to the front of the canoe. Sometimes, a piece of carved cedar was also added to the back. Finally, the canoe was made more watertight by charring it over a fire.

Larger canoes were decorated in part or completely with painted designs. Sometimes the wooden paddles used to propel the canoes were also carved and decorated. These were made waterproof with a coating of grease.

TRADE

Coastal Indians were well established traders long before the first non-Indian traders arrived in their territory. In fact, they were often able to make shrewd deals with the newcomers since they were already so well experienced in the fine points of trade.

In early times native traders used a tooth-shaped mollusk as a form of money all along the Pacific Coast, and inland, as well. This shell, known as dentalium, was found primarily off Vancouver Island. The Nootka gathered it and other tribes obtained dentalium through trade with the Nootka. Blankets were also used as a form of currency. Coastal natives collected blankets in great quantities to display their wealth.

Other items that were valuable for trading purposes among the Indians included the bones and oil of whale, which the Nootka traded. The Tsimshian traded horns of mountain sheep, as well as eulachon oil.

The Haida and the Nootka both made canoes to trade. The Haida also traded red cedar logs (considered superior to yellow cedar logs for some purposes) and carved chests. The Tlingit obtained raw copper from interior Indians and exported it to the south, where the metal was made into ceremonial plaques.

The Makah traded their whale and seal oil, dried herring eggs (known as roe) and other products from the sea to the Nootka for their cedar canoes and planks. They traded their products to other groups for mountain goat meat. Then they traded the meat for red ocher found only in Quileute territory. The ocher was used for cosmetics as well as for war paint.

The Chinook, who lived in the Columbia Valley, further south than any of the tribes mentioned above, brought abalone shells up from Oregon to coastal Indians, who used them to decorate their masks, blankets, and ornaments. It was primarily the Chinook who brought coastal products to the interior tribes, and products from the interior tribes back to the coast.

WAR

While trading was one way to get possessions on the Pacific Northwest Coast, war was another. Some wars were more like small feuds begun over an insult; these could last many years with only a few men killed annually. War chiefs were chosen to lead the battles, and in some groups, one person held this position for many years.

Pacific Northwest Coast warriors wore protective cedar helmets with a carved and painted face meant to scare the enemy. They also wore carved wooden collar bands and armor. The Tlingit made their armor by tying foot-long wooden slats together, then wrapping them around their bodies over vests made out of tough animal hide (such as elk or moose). Another war dress, worn by the Nootka, was a long double-thick skin shirt that was either sleeveless or had only one sleeve.

Weapons were primarily bows and arrows, as well as short spears, and knives. Bows were often made from yew or serviceberry wood, and arrows were made from red cedar. The Tlingit knives were made of bone and were both double-edged and double-bladed. War clubs were also used. These were made from a variety of materials, such as whale's rib, wood, and stone.

There were two main reasons for warfare: to revenge an insult or to take slaves. If a single member of one tribe was insulted, the tribe might seek revenge from the whole tribe to which the insulter belonged.

According to reports, a war was officially declared when a proposal for a war expedition was made public by someone of high rank in a village. A time was set for the expedition's departure. Then the warriors and their wives, as well as the whole community, underwent traditional ceremonies to assure the mission's success.

Crews for the war fleet were organized so that there would be someone responsible for every duty, from watching the canoes in enemy territory to setting fire to houses and securing slaves. The war canoes would arrive at night and attack at dawn, catching their victims asleep.

If the motive was revenge, both sexes were killed. However, if slaves were sought, only the men were killed. The women and children of both sexes were brought back as captives, and the male slave children were allowed to grow into manhood.

BURIAL CEREMONIES

▲ Wooden Indian spirit gravehouses at a Russian Orthodox cemetery near Anchorage, Alaska.

▼ The Raven god adorns this tombstone in a Kwakiutl cemetery on Vancouver Island, British Columbia.

THE IMPORTANCE OF BASKETRY

◀ A woman wears the traditional knob-topped woven basketry hat once only worn by Nootka noblemen.

▲ Flowering heads of tall beargrass, a mountain wildflower that was often used in the weaving of baskets.

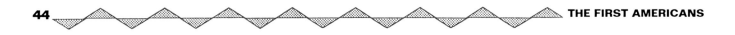

▲ Ed Carrierre, a Squamish (Salish group) Indian, weaves a clam basket on his people's reservation in western Washington. Seattle, once a chief of this tribe, gave his name to the city.

▼ This Nootka coiled cedar bark basket with a lid has a whaling motif.

▶ The skilled hands of a modern Indian artisan weave a coastal-style basket.

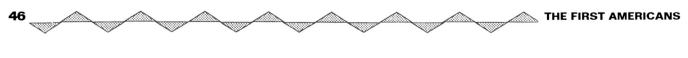

FISHING AND HUNTING

▶ The pelt of the sea otter was valued for its warmth and beauty. These playful animals were nearly made extinct by fur hunters, but today they are protected.

◀ Hunting mountain goats was difficult, but these agile animals were highly valued for their wool, from which blankets were woven, and their horns, from which spoons and dippers were made.

▼ The old traditions continue today. Modern coastal Indians dry salmon on racks in the sun much as their ancestors did centuries ago.

▲ Seals were good to eat and also provided the Indians with a variety of useful objects. The fur was used for warm clothing. After white fur traders entered the area, these animals were hunted nearly to extinction.

CHAPTER THREE

RITUALS AND RELIGION

For the Pacific Northwest Coast Indians the line between the everyday world and a world of spirits was very thin. They shared their lives with many supernatural spirits. They believed that everything, from a pebble on the beach to a mighty grizzly bear, had a spirit. Every person could trace his or her family history to a spirit ancestor. Many of these spirits took on the form of animals. Stories about the spirits were often told by the elders of the tribes during winter evenings, when families and households gathered around their fires.

Some stories explained the origins of specific clans and families. Others explained where the Guardian Spirits came from. However, coastal natives had no creation story. Rather, the world was always here and the stories explain why it exists in its present shape.

Many stories involve a Trickster character who is cunning, lazy, and deceptive. Among the more southern tribes, this role went to Mink and Blue Jay. Among the Tlingit, Tsimshian, and Haida, Raven was the supreme trickster.

Along the coast, the real raven was a common sight. And in the countless tales told about his storied counterpart, the raven brings the world many gifts, but he never does so intention-

ally. Rather, his presents are a result of selfish motives that backfire on him.

According to one famous story, before human beings existed, powerful beings called the Original People lived on the Earth. Although they were immortal, they shared a world of total darkness. But Raven was to change that.

All the light in the world was controlled by one great family, headed by the Sky Chief. Raven was determined to steal this light for himself.

The Sky Chief's close-knit family included a lovely daughter in her teens. Raven decided to become a member of the family by pretending to be the daughter's baby. To do this he turned himself into a tiny needle that came from a hemlock tree. As a needle, Raven got into the girl's water container. When she took a drink of water, Raven got inside her body.

Once there, he began to grow into a baby. The family was puzzled by the girl's unexpected pregnancy, but since they loved her very much, they welcomed her baby when he was born.

This baby boy was actually Raven. He was now one of the family, just as he had plotted.

He began crying constantly, and his wild screams nearly drove everyone crazy. The whole family tried to make him happy. They gave him whatever he wanted, to quiet him down. This included a carved cedar chest that was nearby.

After he had the box, Raven quickly opened it. Starlight fell from it and escaped through a smoke hole in the house to scatter throughout the sky. This was the world's first light.

Raven wanted more. His constant screams made his family try appeasing him again. They gave him the next box he demanded. This, too, Raven opened. Inside it, he found the Moon. He threw the Moon up, and like the starlight, the Moon left through the smoke hole. Now Earth had a light for the nighttime sky.

But Raven had still not found what he wanted the most. He screamed for a third cedar box that was near him. His family, their nerves on edge, gave in to his wishes once more.

One peek and Raven saw that this box contained the Sun. Now he had what he wanted, the most powerful light in the world. He quickly turned himself back into Raven, and with the Sun box in his claws, he flew through the smoke hole, never to return.

The Original People were furious with Raven's trickery. They cursed him for his actions, but their words only made him angry at them. He demanded they stop yelling at him.

When they refused to heed Raven's words, he opened the Sun box. Instantly, brilliant sunlight flooded the world and blasted the Original People in every direction. In this way, they became the land animals, the birds, and the fish we still see today.

There are many variations to this tale, just as there are many more Raven stories. In one of them, all the water in the world belongs to Raven's cousin Petrel, the seabird. So Raven visits him and when Petrel falls asleep, Raven steals the water by filling his beak with it. Then he tries to fly away, the water in his beak and the box, with the Sun, in his claws.

But before the thieving Raven can get very far, Petrel awakes and realizes he's been robbed. He sends his spirit helpers to get Raven. When they catch up to him, Raven can't defend himself, since his beak is filled with water. So he begins spitting the water out, and from his mouth come the lakes, the rivers, and the sea.

In another story Raven creates the Queen Charlotte Islands. This happens at a time when the world is covered with water, and Raven is banished from his sky home. In order for him to have a place to land, he drops the stones he carries, and each one forms an island.

A cycle of legends explain the origin of the many language groups along the Pacific North-west Coast. These are the flood stories. They tell of a time when water covered all of the land and the people had to live in their canoes to survive. This forced them to scatter and settle in different areas, leading to many divisions along the coast.

A favorite myth of the Tsimshian concerns the Grizzly Bear-of-the-Sea, or the Sea Grizzly. According to this story, while fishermen were out on a lake, the giant Sea Grizzly smashed into their boat. The Sea Grizzly had human faces on his fin and human hair. The fishermen killed him with their spears. They cut off the monster's head and much of his hair. They also took his claws. This angered the water spirits who were already angry over a previous insult to the Mountain Goat spirit. To avenge both the Mountain Goat and the Sea Grizzly spirit, the water spirits flooded the land with a sea of foam. The foam kept rising until the fishermen surrendered the Grizzly's hair and claws to the water. However, the fishermen kept the monster's head and remembered him in their totem poles.

The supernatural giant Gunah-kah-daht also figures in a famous myth on the Northwest Coast. The story tells of a great chief who was out in a canoe with his crew, hunting sea otter. Suddenly, a fierce storm came up. Since he was far from shore, the chief feared he would soon meet his doom.

Then Gunah-kah-daht appeared from out of the waves, faced the chief, and vanished beneath the waters again. This supernatural giant was known to help those who looked upon him. The chief had recognized him, and his spirits were lifted. Then many more hours passed, and the chief and his crew wound up shipwrecked on a deserted island. No food could be found, and once again the chief feared that death was near.

Then the chief had an important dream. In it he was told that he and his crew would be saved if he built eight totems of the Keet (also known as the Killer Whale) and threw them into the sea. Before this, the Keet was considered a terrible monster. To be rescued by him seemed absurd. But the chief remembered seeing Gunah-kah-daht, and so he got to work.

After working non-stop, the totems were finally finished—and as soon as the chief threw them into the sea, seals and fish appeared everywhere. The men now had food to eat, and this gave them the strength to build a new canoe and head for home.

To this day the sight of the Keet's dorsal fin is a sign to the Tsimshian that their fishing and

▲ This chief's ceremonial crest hat is painted and carved to represent a bear. A killer whale's fin is at the back.

▲ Even ordinary canoe paddles were carved and decorated. These paddles were made by a Tlingit.

sealing will be crowned with success. As with other myths, there are many versions of this one. Yet, further south, the Killer Whale continues to be an enemy. Winter ceremonies always had dances acting out ancient myths about struggles with Killer Whales. Two more important supernatural figures on the Pacific Northwest Coast are the Serpent and Dzonokwa.

The Nootka believed in a one-headed snake whose scales gave them supernatural powers when hunting the whale. They called this creature Hai-et-lik. The serpent of the Kwakiutl was known as the Sisiutl. This was a two-headed creature with a human face on either end. He could shrink himself to fool people and meeting him almost always meant death.

Dzonokwa, well-known to the Kwakiutl, was a giant female who lived in the woods and kidnapped children to eat them. While Dzonokwa could be very harmful to people, she could also bestow great wealth upon them.

CEREMONIAL AND EVERYDAY ART

Art was as much a part of life here as were the spirits. Everything was adorned, from hats to housefronts. The Pacific Northwest Coast Indians used many art forms but are best known for their intricate wood carvings.

While the majestic totem poles carved by the Pacific Northwest Indians certainly distinguish them, these were only some of the wooden items they skillfully created. Their everyday objects, such as utensils, bowls, fishhooks, and canoe paddles were often beautifully carved with designs. Other wooden items ranged from cedar boxes to tobacco pipes, which began to be carved after the Europeans introduced the habit of smoking tobacco to coastal natives.

The Indians also made a variety of handsomely carved ceremonial masks. These originated out of religious practices, rather than artistic tradition. However, many non-Indians view these spirit masks as art forms.

Some masks were highly elaborate, with two or three faces in one: when the wearer pulled the cords, the outer mask opened up, revealing a second (and sometimes a third) mask inside. These were worn at nighttime ceremonies, when the light was dim, and witnesses couldn't detect the cords. The masks had large carvings designed to scare the audience.

Performers also shook ceremonial wooden rat-

▲ Cedar storage boxes were made by steaming a plank until it was softened and then bending it to form the sides. The seam was sewn together with spruce roots.

tles of different sizes, shapes, and designs. Some had delicately designed figures of people and animals on them. Others, called moon rattles, had a face carved on each side.

Pottery was lacking in this area and the Northwest Coast Indians used boxes in the same way that other American Indian groups used pottery. Their square wooden boxes came in a variety of sizes and served many purposes: from cooking vessels to storage units and burial coffins. Some were carved with the front part of an animal on one end, the rear of the animal on the other end, and the sides of the animal's body on the sides of the box. The creation of these boxes is considered to be one of the special accomplishments of the Pacific Northwest Coast Indians.

The boxes were made by bending one piece of wood with steam, and then joining the final side and bottom with wooden pegs; sometimes spruce roots were sewn through drilled holes instead. Many boxes had heavy wooden covers.

Wood was made into everyday bowls, as well as large ceremonial troughs. Smaller oil dishes were often made in the shape of a seal, with a head carved at one end and a tail carved on the other. These bowls held the eulachon oil into which various fish, meat, and fruits and vegetables were dipped.

Other arts at which the Pacific Northwest Indians were proficient included textiles, which they used to make nets, mats, baskets, and blankets. While men were responsible for carving all the wooden objects, from canoes and chests to totem poles, it was the women who made the textile products. Nets were most often made out of nettle fiber. In many areas, mats were made from the inner bark of cedar, but in the south reeds were sometimes used for making mats. The material had to be kept damp in order to be pliable, and for this purpose a mat maker always kept a container of water by her side. Geometric designs, such as squares and rectangles, were often used for decoration. Among the northern tribes, many mats, as well as blankets, were embroidered with porcupine quills.

Basketry was raised to a high art in this area. Some of the expertly woven baskets here are among the world's finest. Baskets were usually made by twining split spruce roots and then embroidering them with bleached or dyed grasses. Colors came from a variety of sources. For instance, black dye was made from hemlock bark, yellow from tree moss, and purple from huckleberries.

Baskets required different weaving techniques, depending on their use. Baskets for clams had an open weave because they had to be strong, yet allow for water and mud to pass through the walls when the clams were rinsed. Baskets that were intended for cooking required a much tighter weave.

Blankets were made by many people along the coast. The Kwakiutl used the bark of cedar for their blankets and then bordered them with strips of sea otter fur or mountain goat wool. The Coast Salish and the Makah wove woolen blankets from mountain goat wool as well as from the white woolly dogs the Salish raised.

But it was the Chilkat, a Tlingit group, who developed furthest the art of blanket making. Their highly decorated blankets were made out of mountain goat wool and cedar bark. Designs for them were painted by the men on wooden boards. The women copied the designs when weaving the blankets on wooden looms. The same pattern could be used again and again.

The Chilkat blankets were worn on ceremonial occasions and carefully stored away when not in use. They were possessed as shows of wealth by the Chilkat, as well as by most other Northwest Coast tribes.

The Kwakiutl traditional ceremonial blanket is a button blanket. However, cloth was also used for decorating them. Like the buttons, the cloth was obtained through trade. Other blankets were decorated with dentalium shells, as well as cowrie shells and copper. Designs typically depicted crests.

Like blankets, expertly crafted copper shields were important displays of wealth. The coppers were shieldlike plaques with crest designs engraved or hammered on them. Before European contact, the copper for shields came in trade from interior tribes, who found the pure copper lying on the ground, often in dry riverbeds. Later, European sheet copper was used.

A craftsman made a copper by first pounding the metal with a stone to flatten it. He cut out the plaque's distinctive shape by scratching on an outline, then hammering grooves along it to create a sharp ridge on the other side. When this was done, he turned the copper over and used sandstone to rub the ridge until it was cut through. Then the bent-up edges were hammered flat. Decorating was done by cutting grooves into the metal from the front and hammering raised patterns in it from the back.

The massive spiral horns of mountain sheep

▲ Soft but strong, cedar bark had many uses. Here it has been woven into a mat and painted with an intricate wolf design.

were also used to create works of art, primarily the long serving ladles and feast dishes found at potlatches. Although the horns were tough and hard, they could be carved when fresh and wet. The horns could also be softened for shaping by steaming them or boiling them. The horns of mountain goats were used, as well. Although these were too small to be made into bowls or ladles, small spoons could be made from them.

In the late 19th century, a new type of art, created especially for the tourists and merchants who wanted Indian souvenirs, made use of argillite. This fine-grained black shale is found only on the Queen Charlotte Islands. Argillite is soft enough to be easily carved with ordinary woodcarving tools. Haida craftspeople began producing these carvings in the early 19th century. Many were made in replicas of traditional items, such as boxes and totem poles.

TOTEM POLES

More than anything else, the trademark of Pacific Northwest Indian life is the totem pole.

The poles get their name because the carved design of the animals or other creatures that represented each clan was called a crest or totem. The totems were carved on everything a family or a clan owned, from their boxes to their poles.

The free-standing totem poles were probably a development from the earlier house posts used by the Haida. The Haida house posts were made from a big log into which a doorway was carved. This was the only entrance to a Haida home. Passersby instantly knew the status of a house owner by looking at the house post. One or more animals were usually carved on it, each representing another family totem. The taller the pole, the more prestige its owner had.

House interiors were decorated with as many carved house posts as the owner could afford and space allowed. These interior poles served a dual purpose: they supported the house and were engraved with scenes depicting stories about the inhabitants. However, although poles were greatly respected, they weren't religious items; totems were never worshipped.

Only wealthy and respected men were allowed to own a totem pole. The most common poles were the memorial poles. These were built when an old chief died, and a new one was to take his place. A memorial pole both honored the dead chief and confirmed the new chief's position in the community. They had personal and

family crest symbols, as well as Guardian Spirit symbols. Some of the highest poles of all were the Tsimshian memorial poles, which could be 50 feet tall or more. Memorial poles were usually put up at the huge celebrations called potlatches. Some coastal groups honored the wife's lineage by placing her totem on or near the top.

When a chief needed a pole, he commissioned a carver to make it for him. Skilled totem pole carvers could become very wealthy. Some poles took a year or more to finish, and the carver was well paid for his work in blankets, food, and other valuables. The pole owner also had to feed and lodge the carver while he worked. As a carver's reputation grew, chiefs from many miles away would summon him when they wanted a totem pole carved.

Carvers were trained from youth in the skills of their craft. They were deeply religious and had one or more Guardian Spirits to help them in their work. The Tsimshian gitsontk ("people who are excluded") were the best-trained of all carvers. They were also the best paid. The gitsontk carved only the symbols of Guardian Spirits. Their work required great privacy; spying on them was punishable by death. On the other hand, the gitsontk risked death if they made even the smallest mistake.

Before a carver began his work, the village shaman or a village elder educated him about the ancestry and crests of the family who wanted the totem. Then a desirable tree was sought.

The preferred tree for making totem poles from was the red cedar, since its wood is very durable yet is easy to carve. After the chosen tree was felled, it was stripped of its branches and bark. Since they were never wasteful, the Indians stored the bark and later used it to make a variety of items, from ropes to rooftops, and skirts to cradle bedding. Then the log was split. If it was large, fire was used to hollow it out. After the wood was hollowed, it was floated to a construction site near the village. There the carver worked in secrecy, behind a screen.

Before European settlers arrived, tools made from stone or bone were used for every phase of the work. The adze was the early carver's most efficient cutting tool; it left many telltale surface cuts that today serve as indicators of a pole's genuine native origin. Rough sharkskin or other

natural abrasives were used to smooth the wood.

Among the Tsimshian and Tlingit, the carver was supervised by a committee of elders, including a shaman. Like the carver, committee members were housed and fed during the entire time of the carving. They were also well paid for their services. The elders came from the wife's clan. The committee and the chief carefully examined each new symbol that was added to the pole.

Paints were used on the poles. In early times, black and various gray shades were made by mixing charcoal, manganese, or graphite with fish or other animal oils. To produce brown hues, as well as reds or whites, ochers of these colors were mixed. Reds came from berries or animal blood mixed with oils. A bright yellow was obtained from a decayed fungus growth. Green came from mixing flakes of copper-containing rocks with animal fats and oils, and purple was made from dark berries.

As well as memorial poles, housefront poles, and house posts, many other poles were common, such as grave figures, mortuary poles, and welcome figures. A grave figure indicated the location of a burial. A mortuary pole contained the remains of the dead. It was used primarily by the Haida. Welcome figures were most popular among the Nootka. These figures seldom had totem symbols. They were situated at the edge of the water along the coast or on an inland stream. By looking at them travelers knew who owned the beach. When guests arrived by canoe for ceremonies, they found their way because of the welcome figures. Among the Haida and Tlingit, there were also ridicule or shame poles, which were used to insult another person, especially one who had not paid his debts. These poles depicted the person's failure to live up to his obligations. Sometimes they were carved upside down, especially if the person guilty of owing a debt was a non-Indian.

Once the early traders arrived, the Indians exchanged their fur pelts (mainly from sea otter) for iron and steel tools. These new tools allowed carvers to work with greater ease and greater speed. Totem pole carving flourished. However, few poles from this period are left standing today, rot and vandalism having taken their toll.

THE POTLATCH

The word *potlatch* comes from the Chinook words for "to give away," which were adopted in turn from the Nootka word *patshatl*, which

◄ A handsome totem pole towers over a Haida house at Skidegate Inlet in British Columbia.

▲ A potlatch is in progress in this photograph of a Kwakiutl village, taken in 1875.

▲ Chilkat Indians gather for a potlatch in Alaska in 1895.

means "a gift." These were social affairs and festivals at which immense amounts of presents were given to the guests, large quantities of food were eaten, and the host's wealth and reputation were displayed. Small-scale potlatches as well as lavish ones were held all year round. The most lavish lasted for many days and nights. The Kwakiutl were noted for holding the most elaborate potlatches of all.

The festivals were held throughout the coastal region to celebrate many different events. These included the building of a new house and the winning of a battle. Funeral potlatches were held, especially among the Tlingit. At funeral potlatches, the life of the deceased chief was recounted. Small potlatches were held to honor

marriages, births, and children coming of age. A potlatch was also a time for boys and girls who had come of age to be initiated into secret societies and for babies to be named.

One of the most important reasons to hold a potlatch was to celebrate the raising of a new totem pole. But, regardless of why a specific potlatch was held, it was always an occasion at which a host repaid others for their services. (Among the Tlingit, the whole clan rather than a single household was the host.)

Long before the big event, the host began making and collecting gifts to give away at it. If he needed more gifts than he had, he asked members of his clan or related clans to help out.

The pole owner also commissioned a songwriter to write songs and gather together performers for the potlatch. Rehearsals began that could last for many weeks or months. The song-

writer worked closely with the shaman to make sure that the songs he composed accurately told the stories of the chief's family. Talented songwriters were greatly respected.

It was the wife's task to prepare the feast for the potlatch. This often included smoked salmon and venison as well as bear meat (except in some areas where eating bear was taboo), berries, and roots. Smoked salmon, braided in strips, was very popular as a kind of candy. A popular drink known as soop-a-lallie was also served. This was made by mixing soapberries and eulachon oil with water.

Among the more southern groups, welcome figures marked the host's beach. Elsewhere, the host or his assistants greeted the invited guests as they docked.

Personal position among the guests was very important even before they stepped ashore. Although they had come from as far away as a hundred miles, they waited to land until they could disembark in their order of rank. The size of canoes was also significant; the greater the chief, the larger his canoe and the more people he came with. Some guests brought along slaves, who paddled their canoes for them.

Once at the ceremonial grounds, people mingled with each other, to retell generations-old stories, and learn the latest news. They also enjoyed games of chance and various performances. And they ate enormous amounts of food.

The mood was festive, but should a guest feel insulted, the mood could camouflage future trouble. Insults came about in many ways, from a guest feeling he wasn't given enough food to thinking that the performances weren't good enough. The result of an insult could be war. Equally serious, the host could be removed from the guest list for the next potlatch.

For much of the potlatch, the recently built totem pole remained hidden. Finally, the time came to unveil it. The guests sat in order of rank as the pole was brought to the location prepared for it. Guests helped hoist up the pole with ropes that were attached to it. Meanwhile, performers sang. Then it was the dancers' job to stomp the dirt down firmly around the pole.

While all this was going on, the host and his kinspeople listened carefully to what guests said about the pole and him. Admiring words were

CEREMONIAL CLOTHING

Traditional Tlingit dancers wear beautifully decorated Chilkat blankets. They are also wearing elaborately decorated hats and clothing. The Indians of the Pacific Northwest Coast were very concerned with personal status. Their ceremonial clothing reflected their wealth.

welcome. But any insulting remarks could result in future wars.

After the pole was secured in the ground, the chief or his spokesperson would make a speech. The speaker wore a ceremonial robe and headdress. In his speech, he explained what each crest and figure on the new pole meant.

Dancers and singers later reenacted the great events the speaker recounted. Then a nephew, chosen by the chief, was introduced as his successor someday. (After the chief died, his nephew would hold a memorial potlatch just as the chief was holding one today.)

The potlatch was still not over. After the initiation of youngsters into the secret societies and the naming of babies, the gift-giving could take place. As the potlatch neared its end, the gifts were brought out of concealment. Among them were blankets, robes, and tools. As each gift was displayed, its value was announced publicly.

The host's family gave out the gifts to their guests in proportion to each guest's wealth, with the wealthiest man receiving the most valuable gift(s). People noticed what each guest received and how it compared with the gifts that guest had given away at earlier potlatches. If a man thought that the gift he received was less than he deserved, his whole family felt insulted.

Once again, warfare could result. Just as likely, the insulted family could give their own potlatch at which they presented the man who had insulted them with a gift meant to insult him in return.

Potlatches were also an occasion for the purchasing or "killing" of coppers. A copper plaque's value was measured in terms of thousands of blankets. Coppers were purchased at a potlatch and then hung on the owner's wall to show his wealth. Every time a copper was newly purchased, its value grew. Coppers were "killed" by throwing them in a fire or in the sea. By such acts, a man was saying that he was wealthy enough to destroy his copper without a care. Coppers could also be broken. However, this was done with great ritual and required five potlatches to perform.

Some potlatches were held to right old wrongs. At these, a person who had previously been insulted would receive the first gift and the grandest gift.

WINTER CEREMONIES

The Pacific Northwest Coast Indians felt that the spirits were always with them. However, it was believed that winter was the easiest time to make contact with them. Winter was also the time when the people could relax, now that their hunting, fishing, gathering, and preserving of food was done for the cold months ahead.

Throughout the coastal region, the major ceremonies were held at this time of year. These were known as the Winter Ceremonies and included the initiation of young people into secret societies, the payment of various debts (such as potlatch and marriage), and many feasts.

Coastal Indians belonged to a variety of Dancing Societies. These societies were most elaborate among the Indians who lived farthest north. The dances of the Tlingit, the Tsimshian, and the Haida were all derived from the Kwakiutl. Salish tribes on the north of Vancouver Island also can be linked to Kwakiutl influence. The Winter Ceremonies required dancers to wear special carved face masks that represented the dancers' spirits or ancestors of the particular society.

Among the Coast Salish, where rank had less importance than further north, winter was the time for people to try securing power from the spirits of their choice. But sometimes the spirits came uninvited. These invisible intruders could suddenly possess people and send them into trances. This was known as spirit sickness. There was only one cure for it. The people had to let their emotions free through Spirit Dancing.

Many dancers were inspired to perform, one after another, around the Long House. Drumming accompanied them as they acted out their spirit. Dancers leapt and danced around, often with wild frenzy. Although no special costume was required, the dancers painted their faces, and carried a symbol of their spirit power with them.

Kwakiutl ceremonies were much more formalized and elaborate. During their Winter Ceremony of Tsitsika (which means "time when nothing is real") new members were initiated into the Kwakiutl Dancing Societies. At such times, members of the tribe could only be called by their winter ceremonial names. Status now changed to one based on a ranked order of spirits and Dancing Societies. Among the Kwakiutl there were many Dancing Societies, each with its own dances to perform. Belonging to such groups was based on inheritance.

The most prestigious Kwakiutl Dancing Society was the Shamans Society, which was made up of shamans and other highly regarded members of the tribe. Their most esteemed dancers

▲ The design painted on this wooden drum symbolizes an owl.

were the Cannibal Dancers, or Hamatsa. The Hamatsa's spirit was the Cannibal-at-the-North-End-of-the-World.

During Kwakiutl Winter Ceremonies, the initiates to the Shamans Society became the main performers and were introduced to the rest of the people. Other society members also did their dances at this time.

The celebration at which the Cannibal Dancers performed began with the blowing of whistles by Hamatsa members in the morning. These whistles produced an eerie sound and were kept in secret when not in use.

Then the young men and women initiates were captured and taken away. They were said to have gone to the house of the Cannibal-at-the-North-End-of-the-World. Actually, they were taken into the woods or the back of a house.

When they returned, they were in ceremonial costume, and under the influence of the Cannibal, a powerful flesh-eating spirit. The initiates bit people on their arms. Then came another secret society, the Bear-men. Its members growled like bears and went on a rampage, destroying people's property. Special society members followed the Hamatsa and the Bear-men to keep track of what property was destroyed so that it could be replaced.

Now the initiates had to be subdued by established society members. This took place both publicly and privately, and an initiate didn't actually become a member of the society for as long as four years.

The public part took place at night in the village's ceremonial house. There, in frenzied performances, the Cannibal Dancers acted out the stories of their ancestors. They wore painted masks that were elaborate art pieces. Some masks resembled birds with giant beaks, such as the supernatural Raven. The beaks could snap open and shut. Other masks had two or three faces in one, so that a dancer could transform himself by pulling its strings. Many of these multiple-face masks had copper on them, perhaps as eyes, or bands on the forehead. Performers also wore ceremonial costumes, often with hanging shredded cedar bark.

The most important ceremony among the Nootka tribes is known as Logwana. It is based on an origin story in which an ancestor visits the House of the Wolves. There he is taught songs and dances. He thinks he has been gone for four days, but he returns home to discover that he has been missing for four years.

The Nootka Wolf Dance dramatizes this story. It began with the capturing of a group of boys by kidnappers wearing wolf disguises.

There was humor in the ceremony, with the parents sometimes being tossed into the sea as punishment for not keeping closer watch on their children. Search parties were formed, and people went around the village, waking everyone up and asking if anyone knew where the young men had been taken. The searches proved fruitless, of course. The next step was to use ceremonial dancing and drumming to lure the Wolves from their hiding place.

A drum leader climbed up to the roof of the ceremonial house to watch for the youngsters and lead the drumming. There was gaiety here, too, with the drum leader insisting that he couldn't hear any drums, even when dozens were beating around him. Eventually the drumming was successful, and the villagers heard the children before they were taken away by their captors once again.

Now a group of villagers devised traps to catch the Wolves. They set out in canoes with others from the village. When the people saw the Wolves on the opposite shore, they pretended to panic. In their excitement they threw the trap-makers overboard.

Once the boats reached the shore, the trap-makers tried to save the youngsters. Instead, they tripped over their own feet and became entangled in their own traps. However, the boggled rescue mission proved successful just the same. It distracted the Wolves, and left the young men unguarded, with enough time to make their escape. The boats departed, leaving behind the trap-makers, who returned later on.

When the children were safely home once more, they repeated the songs and dances they had learned from the Wolves. The festivities ended with a potlatch.

SHAMANS

Throughout the Pacific Northwest Coast, the most powerful spirit of all was believed to belong to the medicine people, or shamans (a word of Russian origin). This was an unsought spirit that could take possession of women as well as men. Anyone who possessed it was both honored and feared in the community.

If a child exhibited special traits that suggested he or she might be a future shaman, the child's parents might take him or her to see the

village shaman. Should the shaman deem him or her worthy, the child would become the shaman's student. This honor would cost the family a hefty price. But it was considered a worthwhile one, because the family's status would greatly increase.

In different groups, the shaman had different specialties. Some shamans specialized in diagnosing a problem. Some healed sicknesses with a combination of rituals, medicine, and spiritual magic. Some assisted in cases of soul loss by traveling to the spirit villages and retrieving lost souls. Others were believed to have powers over external events, such as war and peace, and the weather. They would perform special ceremonies to assure that the wishes of the tribe were met. War parties didn't leave without first getting the ceremonial blessing and advice of the shaman. Shamans also officiated at funeral rites.

A family would call a shaman to cure a family member after their own herbs and magic failed to work. The cause of disease was often thought to be an object that was sent into the victim's body by a person or spirit who was angry with him or her. The shaman had to find the alien object and remove it.

A curing ritual was required, during which the patient's relatives were present. Shamans used the sucking cure to remove a disease from the afflicted area. They sucked out the alien object through a long bone or wooden tube. They also employed herbs, potions, small figures, and carved charms that sometimes hung from their clothes. Rattles were also used, as well as a series of different headdresses and masks. Hidden devices and sleight-of-hand might also be a part of the shaman's "medicine."

Other times soul loss was the problem, and soul retrieval was prescribed. Among the northernmost tribes, the shaman went into a deep trance that sent him or her into a frenzy. The shaman would often yell and bite spectators as he or she mentally journeyed to the spirit villages to find and bring back the patient's wandering soul. Sometimes shamans used a device known as a soul-catcher, which was made out of bone or ivory.

Among the Coast Salish, painted boards were erected to represent spirit canoes. The shaman took a pantomime journey in them to the Land of the Dead. Among the Nootka, the shaman physically went on a hunt. The trip was believed to take the shaman under the sea. Assistants tied a line around the shaman's waist to make sure that he or she got home safely.

Shamans sometimes waged battle with each other. These battles required no physical contact. Instead, the shamans tried using their spirits to kill those of their rival. They also fought each other with insults by using their rival's name in place of regular words. For instance, a shaman might say "I'm hungry. I want to eat [a rival's name]."

MEDICINAL PLANTS

Like Indians throughout North America, Pacific Northwest Coast natives knew much about the medicinal qualities of the plants in their area. They used a variety of plants to help heal the sick. Some plants were known only to the shamans, but others were known to the people.

The Haida used the bark of lodgepole pine as a cast or splint. The Bella Coola heated its sap and applied it to sore joints. Spider webs were used to stop bleeding. Wounds were bound with strips of bitter cherry bark. Strips of the inner bark of yellow cedar were used as tourniquets.

The stems of devil's club were allowed to rot, then burned to ashes and mixed with fish oil or spruce pitch as a lotion for sores. The leaves of the western skunk cabbage were used as a poultice. (A poultice is a soft, wet, absorbent pad.)

The Bella Coola and others used the mashed root of western dock, as well as the powdered toasted leaves of black birch and wintergreen, on cuts and boils. Another aid for cuts and other wounds was the bark of the pussy willow.

Indians of this area made a tea from the root of the dandelion for stomach pain. They used juniper as a cough medicine. Some also used a concoction made with lady fern to cure coughs and chest pains. The Bella Coola used lady fern in an eyewash.

BELIEFS OF THE NORTHWEST COAST NATIVE AMERICANS

▼ · ▼ · ▼ · ▼ · ▼ · ▼ · ▼ · ▼ · ▼

TOTEM POLES

▲ The "Hole in the Ice" totem pole, at least 90 years old, once served as the ceremonial entrance to a Tsimshian village house. The hole is surrounded by 12 small human figures.

◀ Beautifully carved totem poles adorned every village in the Pacific Northwest, proclaiming the heritage of the residents.

▶ Totem poles were carved from big cedar logs, sanded smooth, and then painted.

▼ The effects of harsh weather and vandalism have faded and toppled many totem poles. In some cases, people have been able to restore them.

LEGENDARY CREATURES

◀ The bald eagle played a role in Native American legends of the region. It is often found carved on top of totem poles.

▶ The raven has been immortalized as a hero-trickster in many legends along the Pacific Northwest Coast.

▼ The killer whale appears in many Pacific Northwest Indian stories. The Haida considered these marine mammals to be the greatest of all living things.

RITUAL OBJECTS

▶ This carved ivory soul-catcher was used by a Kitksan shaman to retrieve the soul of someone who was ill because his or her soul was lost.

◀ Human faces and whales are shown on this ancient petroglyph (rock carving) near Cape Alava, now part of Olympic National Park in Washington.

▼ Intricate wooden masks such as this one, made by a Bella Coola craftsman, were carved and then painted. Many of these masks were quite elaborate and had movable parts.

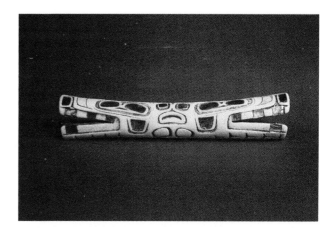

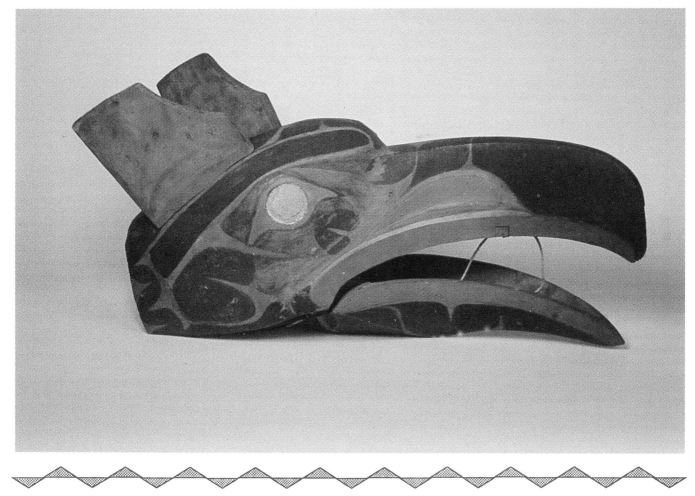

▲ The beautifully crafted Tlingit copper has a bear design painted on it.

CHAPTER FOUR

CHANGE

ntil the 16th century, natives of the Pacific Northwest Coast had no idea that white-skinned people existed in the world. They also knew very little about the Indians living beyond the coastal mountains that isolated them from the rest of North America and its inhabitants. But that all began to change in 1579. In that year, Francis Drake, the first Englishman to sail around the world, reached what is now northern California. Queen Elizabeth had sent him on a mission to find a sea passage through North America—the elusive Northwest Passage.

With his ship in need of repair, Drake landed north of present-day San Francisco. There he met the Miwok Indians, who were friendly to Drake and let him stay with them while he worked on his ship, the *Golden Hind.*

He was the first European known to have sailed that far north along the Pacific Northwest Coast, and he claimed it for England. After five weeks in California, he returned home with the first reports ever received in that part of the globe about the people of the Pacific Coast. He named the land he had reached "New Albion" (Albion was the ancient Greek word for England).

It wasn't until nearly 200 years later that other explorers would return to the area. In the 1700s non-Indians began arriving in large numbers. Soon, the life of the Northwest Coast Indians would be drastically changed, and a centuries-old way of life would be nearly destroyed.

In the 17th and 18th centuries, Spain and England were the most energetic explorers for new territories. Spain had made many conquests in Mexico but had not landed as far north along the coast as Drake. For a long time the English did not return.

In 1728, a Dane named Vitus Bering, sailing under the patronage of the Russian czar, discovered the sea route between Siberia and Russia. (Now known as the Bering Strait, this same route had served as a land bridge during the Ice Age, allowing the first Americans to reach the New World by crossing it.)

In 1740, Bering returned for another expedition. During this voyage, he discovered Kayak, an island close to what is now the Alaskan mainland, and the crew on one of his ships became the first Europeans to venture ashore. However, the crew never returned, and were presumably killed by the Tlingit, since a group of war canoes approached Bering's ship and threatened it. Bering sailed away and during his return voyage was shipwrecked and died. His own crew made it back to Siberia, where they told the czar about the region they had discovered. What most impressed them were the furs they had found, especially the silky sea otter pelts. These came to be known in Russia as "soft gold."

The czar, excited by the stories, wanted to colonize the area for Russia. Independent fur hunters and trappers from Russia set out in search of the riches awaiting them there. Most of these men weren't sailors, nor were they very good at hunting sea otters. Some of them forced the Aleut, who lived on what we now call the Aleutian Islands (north of Tlingit territory) to hunt the swift-moving animals for them. The Aleut had much better boats for the region than the Russians did. These boats were covered with animal skin and were known as kayaks.

The Aleut were masters at hunting sea otter. In fact, the animals soon became nearly extinct in their waters. The Russians now wanted to extend their hunting range further south. After getting the reports back from a naval expedition sent out to find a good site to settle, the Russians chose to put up a trading post on what is today known as Baranov Island, off the southern strip of Alaska.

In 1799 Alexander Baranov, a Russian, led a small fleet of boats and kayaks to the island that now bears his name. Aleut were part of his crew. However, this new territory belonged to their enemies, the Tlingit.

Even before the Russians and Aleut reached their destination, they had battles with the Tlingits. However, they would not turn back. When they were safely ashore at what is today Sitka, Alaska, the Russians met with the Tlingit. Baranov told them that he was interested in trading, and not fighting, with them. The Tlingit doubted Baranov's good intentions, but they let him and his people remain.

The Russians and Aleut built a fort for themselves called New Archangel. But things quickly went downhill. The Russians were unable to keep their promise of trade with the Tlingit, since Russian supply ships did not come their way very often. Therefore, the Russians had little to offer in trade. In fact, they barely had enough supplies for themselves.

The situation got worse and worse. Finally, on a Sunday afternoon in June of 1802, over a thousand Indians, most of them Tlingit, attacked New Archangel. Since many of New Archangel's inhabitants (including Baranov) were away for the day, the fort could not be adequately defended.

When word reached Moscow about the massacre of Russian settlers in Alaska, the Russian czar immediately ordered an attack upon the Indians in retaliation. It took two years before the Russians were ready to strike. By then, the Tlingit had control of the fort.

But when the huge Russian warship equipped with giant cannons was spotted by them, the Tlingit panicked and put their weapons down. They began many days of talks with Baranov, who was on board the heavily armed ship.

Then one day there was an unnatural quiet about the fort. The Tlingit had sneaked away during the night. To prevent any noise from tipping off the Russians about their plan, they had killed their own children and dogs and left their bodies behind.

After that, the Russians built a new and larger fort elsewhere on Baranov Island, and a few years later, they built another colony on Yakutat Bay. This was in Tlingit territory. When the Tlingit destroyed it, the Russians decided not to rebuild it.

The big fort on Baranov Island remained, but an uneasy peace existed between the Russians and Tlingit. And, as time went on, competition from the Americans, the Canadians, and the British made it hard for Russian traders to sell their furs profitably. Russia's influence on the Pacific Northwest Coast began to decrease rapidly.

In 1824 and 1825, Russia signed treaties with the United States and Great Britain that recognized latitude 54° 40' as the southern boundary of Russian claims in America. Russia gave the United States and Britain the right to trade along Alaska's Pacific coast. In 1867, the United States purchased Alaska from Russia for $7.2 million, and the Indians living there came under the jurisdiction of the United States.

The Spanish and English continued their rivalry for control of North America. However, it was in response to the Russian expansion in the area that Spain sent a Spanish ship to the Northwest Coast in 1774. The navigator, Juan Perez, traveled as far as the Queen Charlotte Islands and made contacts with the natives, but he did not land.

Further south, the Spanish had been expanding their presence in California since 1769. They would eventually build 21 missions there. These missions, as well as forts, were erected with the forced labor of Indians who were made to give up their life-style and work for the soldiers and clergymen of Spain.

But it was the English who would go down in history as the first Europeans to land along the

▲ In the early 1800s, Alexander Baranov led the settlement of Russian fur traders in New Archangel, which is today Sitka, Alaska.

Northwest Coast. The man who lead the landmark expedition was Captain James Cook.

By 1778 Captain Cook had already become the first European to visit New Zealand and the Cook Islands on two previous voyages to the Pacific. On this trip, before arriving on the Pacific Northwest Coast, he reached the island of Hawaii, which was inhabited by the descendants of its Polynesian settlers.

Cook's two ships were named the *Discovery* and the *Resolution*. They traveled along the coast of Washington State, encountering fierce storms that lasted for weeks. Finally they found shelter on Vancouver Island, in what has come to be called Nootka Sound.

There they were immediately met by Nootka in three canoes. Some of the Indians gave speeches in a language that Cook's crew couldn't understand, while they shook rattles at the same time. One of the men seemed to be the leader. In Cook's words, he was painted "in an extraordinary manner." Although none of the men came on board Cook's ships, they were eager to trade.

The next day, more canoes came within close range of the English ships, but no Indians accepted the crew's offer to come on board until

▲ This combined trading post and fort was built by Alexander Baranov on an island he named for himself.

the third day. After that, there were daily visits by the Nootka, and a brisk trade developed. Both sides communicated with each other in sign language. The Indians traded furs of many animals for anything made out of metal, from nails to knives. The Nootka also were eager to trade their furs for buttons and mirrors. Cook's crew purchased the furs, expecting to make them into clothing when they got back home.

In the meantime, while Cook's ships underwent repair, he was welcomed into many Nootka households, and his journals give us a good description of the people of Nootka Sound. (Cook at first named the harbor King George Sound, in honor of his king, but later learned that the natives called it Nootka Sound.)

After several weeks, Cook's ships were ready to sail on. As the captain took leave of Nootka Sound, he received many invitations to return again. But Cook was now intent on sailing further north to find the Northwest Passage. And wherever he went, he continued to trade with the Indians and to carefully map the coastline. His ships traveled around Alaska and sailed into the Arctic Ocean.

Then they sailed westward, back to Hawaii again, where Cook died in a quarrel with native islanders. However, his crew continued to sail on to China. There, Cook's sailors discovered that the Chinese valued sea otter fur and paid extremely high prices for the pelts.

Since the crew had bought the furs for practically nothing, the profits were enormous. When the men returned to England, their news about the desirable furs on the Northwest Coast quickly spread throughout Europe. Word of the fortunes to be made in trading Northwest Coast furs to the Chinese was also heard in the United States, which had become an independent country in 1776. Merchants from Europe and the United States began heading for the coastal lands.

The coastal Indians came to call the British "King George's men," the Spanish "King Carlos's men," and the Americans "Boston men," since most seemed to come from that city.

The Indians' early trade with the newcomers introduced them to many items they desired, and relationships between Indians and traders were friendly. However, between the newcomers there were often disputes.

In 1789 there was a major confrontation between the Spanish and English at Nootka Sound. At this time, the Spanish had control of the harbor. One of their ships was present, as well as an English ship and an American vessel, when the conflict broke out.

Apparently, the Spanish captain was following his orders, which were to explore the Pacific coast and drive away any foreign ships. Therefore, he felt justified in taking the captain and crew of the British ship as captives. When a second British ship arrived, the Spanish also took the sailors on this ship as prisoners.

The Nootka, who were especially friendly to the English, were furious at the treatment of their friends. The chief's own brother sailed toward the Spanish ship with his wife and child, shouting curses at the Spanish. Suddenly, there was a loud sound and the cursing stopped. The chief's brother had been killed by the Spanish.

The Nootka wanted revenge, but the chief held them back. He feared that many more Indians would die in a battle, since their weapons were no match for the Spaniards' guns. Instead, he led his people away to a new site located where the Spanish ships could not enter. The next year, the Spanish ships returned to find that the entire village was empty.

The British wanted more than their ships and men returned. They also demanded the right to set up a permanent trading post at Nootka Sound. The Spanish took the demand as a direct challenge to their control of the area. However, they knew that the British navy was strong, and should they lose a battle here, they might be forced to surrender other colonies to England. Rather then risk a possible defeat to England, Spain gave in to the British demands.

In 1792 the two countries signed a treaty that came to be called the Nootka Agreement. The treaty granted all nations the right to trade with Indians along the Pacific Coast north of the California missions.

The most immediate result of the Nootka Agreement was that many more ships from many more countries now came to the area to trade, including a great number from the United States.

In 1792, the same year Spain and England signed the Nootka Agreement, an American became the first white man to reach the mouth of the Columbia River. Captain Robert Gray named the river after his ship, the *Columbia*.

Twelve years later, soon after the American purchase of the Louisiana Territory from France, President Thomas Jefferson despatched Captain Meriwether Lewis and his friend William Clark on an expedition. Officially, Lewis and Clark were to lead a survey of the newly purchased territory. They were also supposed to establish friendly relations with the Indians. But Jefferson wanted more than that. His plans were for the party to go as far as the Pacific Ocean and claim the land for the United States.

In part, Jefferson was influenced by his talks some years earlier with John Ledyard, an American writer and fur trader. Ledyard had sailed with Captain Cook to Nootka Sound and had published his journal of the voyage in 1783.

Almost two years after the Lewis and Clark expedition set out in May of 1804, the exhausted party reached the Pacific. There were 45 people in all, including one woman, a Shoshoni Indian guide named Sacajawea.

At the mouth of the Columbia River they encountered the Chinook Indians, just as Captain Gray had in 1792.

Lewis and Clark set up their camp on the south shore of the Columbia River. They called it Fort Clatsop for the Clatsop Chinook Indians who lived in the area and were helpful and friendly to the newcomers.

The Chinook traded with Americans, Europeans, and Indians. They developed a kind of trade language that became known as "Chinook jargon" and incorporated words in various foreign languages.

The United States felt that the Lewis and Clark expedition, along with Captain Gray's discovery, gave the young country as solid a claim to the Pacific as those of Spain, Britain, and Russia. In 1811 they set up an American trading post about eight miles away from Fort Clatsop.

The new post, the first permanent settlement in Oregon Territory, would become the state's first city. It was named Astoria, in honor of its founder, John Jacob Astor. (Astor's group, the Pacific Trade Company, later set up the first permanent settlement in Washington State.)

Astoria's inhabitants quickly began trading

▲ Meriwether Lewis (left) and William Clark (right) led the first exploration by whites of the Columbia River and the territory that is now Oregon and Washington in the early 1800s.

with the Indians. But it wasn't long before Astoria ran into serious trouble. When war broke out between the United States and Britain in 1812, Astoria's fur traders feared that they couldn't successfully defend the post against the British. So Astoria was sold to a British Canadian fur company in 1813, just two years after it was first established. This strengthened the Canadian presence in the Pacific Northwest.

The Canadians had prior claims to the area. In 1793, Alexander Mackenzie, a Canadian of Scottish descent, became the first non-Indian to cross the northern part of the North American continent to the Pacific, which he reached at Bella Coola. He charted the Pacific coast for Canada. Besides reaching the longest river in Canada, which now bears Mackenzie's name, he was also a partner in the Northwest Fur Company of Canada. The company was primarily interested in the trading of beaver furs.

In 1821, the company was bought out by their main rival, the Hudson's Bay Company, which had been started in 1670. As the Hudson's Bay's explorers traveled inland to find new sources of furs, they helped open Canada to settlement from Hudson Bay all the way to the Pacific Ocean. The combined companies retained the name of Hudson's Bay Company. (The company still exists today as the world's largest fur-trading firm.)

It is from this company that the coastal Indians bought trade blankets in great quantities. These replaced the blankets that they once used to weave by hand.

As for Astoria, its name was changed to Fort George, in honor of the British king, and for many years it was considered the region's major center for trade by both the Indians and foreigners to the land.

In the early 1800s, Russia claimed Alaska, based on the country's earlier explorations there. However, as the sea otter diminished in number, the appeal of the land also lessened. In 1824 and 1825 Russia signed treaties with Great Britain and the United States, giving up its interests south of latitude 54° 40'. Even earlier than that, in 1819, Spain signed a treaty giving up its claim north of latitude 42°, which is Oregon's present southern boundary.

But the United States and Britain could not agree on a boundary line between their claims. While they continued debating where it should be, they signed treaties in 1818 and again in 1827 that permitted both countries to trade and settle in the region, called the Oregon Country.

By the 1820s, the sea otter was greatly depleted in all the Pacific waters off Canada and Alaska. By now the fur had also ceased to be a rarity in China. At the same time, the trade in furs of other animals increased. These included the beaver, marten, land otter, and mink.

In 1824, the Hudson's Bay Company, which had used Fort George as its main trading post, moved farther up the Columbia River to establish Fort Vancouver, their first coastal site. Slowly, a small community of white men, many with Indian wives and families, began settling around Fort Vancouver.

Word quickly spread about the rich farmland they found in the area, known as Willamette Valley. Scores of new settlers, mainly Americans, began arriving. They endured great hardships to come by land. In 1843 the first great overland migration into Oregon doubled the number of white people in the region. After that, settlers by the hundreds arrived every year.

Before many years, Oregon had many more Americans than Canadians or British. At the same time, the Indians were being squeezed off their own lands; their hunting grounds disappeared as the new settlers cut down trees and cleared the land for farming. Finding it hard to fight, the natives wound up living solely off the foods they could find along the coast, which was not suitable as farmland.

In 1846 President James Polk signed a treaty with Great Britain that fixed the 49th parallel as the chief dividing line between U.S. and British claims. Great Britain kept Vancouver Island, part of which lies south of the 49th parallel.

In 1848, Oregon became a territory. In 1853, the Washington Territory, which consisted of the present state of Washington, northern Idaho, and western Montana, was created. At that time, Oregon's present boundaries were established.

The territory's first governor, Isaac Ingalls Stevens, signed many treaties with the coastal Indians, which put them on reservations. The treaties generally took away large chunks of traditional Indian homelands in return for services, such as schools and medical care.

Trade with the Europeans, Russians, and Americans caused many changes in the coastal Indians' way of life.

From their earliest days of contact, the Indians began to use many of the non-Indians' more efficient and robust tools, which were made out of iron and steel. The many carefully made everyday tools they had used for years began to be replaced by strong, cheap tools that the foreigners brought. With their new axes and saws they could chop down trees more quickly than ever. The new steel hammers and chisels now available enabled them to build canoes, houses, masks, and totem poles more easily than before.

At first, the increased productivity now possible afforded some of the coastal Indians greater wealth than ever. The richer families got richer. However, the poorer families got poorer, since they had nothing to trade with the merchants who sailed into their ports.

At the same time, trading affected the old Indian ways. Many customs were forgotten as the Indians began concentrating on hunting sea otter and other animals for trade. The tradition of making blankets by hand nearly became extinct now that the Hudson's Bay Company brought quantities of cheap woolen blankets to trade.

But there was more. The spirit of the people weakened tremendously as the villages experienced epidemics that wiped out families and even whole villages.

Along with goods to trade, the Europeans also brought to the Pacific Northwest tragic sicknesses. These included measles, tuberculosis, and smallpox. The Native Americans lacked the natural immunities that the Europeans had built up to many of these diseases. When they struck, they quickly swept through an area and took many lives.

Among the Chinook Indians, a major epidemic began in the early 1830s when a Chinook Indian mysteriously contracted a strange disease after picking up something in the harbor where British ships were docked. Nothing could ease the man's sweating, shivering, and fever. The shaman was summoned, but he could not save the patient. Soon the sick man died. Then others in his village began showing similar symptoms. They too died.

The "cold sick," as it was called, quickly spread from one Indian village to another.

Sometimes a whole village was wiped out by illness in hours. Today, we suspect that the cold sick was a kind of influenza. Like other imported diseases, it proved deadly to the Indians.

Along the coast, the most dramatic impact was upon the Haida. They numbered 6,000 in 1835, and less than 600 by 1915. A great smallpox epidemic had struck them in 1862. It began in the Vancouver Island town of Victoria, which the Hudson's Bay Company moved to in 1849. Victoria became a boom town soon after gold was discovered on the Queen Charlotte Islands in 1852. The news about gold started a great influx of immigrants, primarily from Great Britain.

In one year, 1858, Victoria went from being a village of 300 to a town of 3,000 permanent settlers, with 6,000 other people camping around it. Many Native Americans, especially Haida, began migrating to the prosperous city every year. They lived in slums on its outskirts, and the attitude of the settlers toward them was derogatory. The newcomers did not see that they were in large part responsible for the plight of the Indians they had replaced. Rather, they saw the Haida and others as obstacles to progress, and they demanded that the government remove them.

But before the problem could be solved by law, smallpox struck in epidemic proportions. As the disease spread through the Indian population of Victoria, the authorities took this as a just cause to evict them and destroy their homes. The Indians returned to their homelands, taking the epidemic with them and causing more deaths.

As a result of this terrible epidemic, the Northwest Coast Indians' population may have been reduced by as much as one-third. In many places, villages were empty of people. Elsewhere, village chiefs died and competition arose to replace them. All over, people died so quickly that there was no time to pass on their heritage to whatever children remained. It was a terrible period for the coastal tribes.

During their early days of contact, the foreigners and coastal Indians were partners in trade. The results seemed positive for everyone. Trade led to a rapid increase in the personal wealth of Indians as well as of non-Indians. Among the Indians, nobody had to spend years making goods by traditional methods for their potlatches. If they had enough furs to trade, they received many valuable objects. As time went on and many old chiefs died in epidemics, more and more potlatches were held to honor the new chiefs. The potlatches were also a way for the

people to hold on to whatever tradition was left.

The Kwakiutl held the most elaborate potlatches of all. In order to show how rich they were, they began burning more and more of their property. Great piles of possessions went up in smoke in front of their homes. Then, the next family to hold a potlatch burned even more possessions than the last.

The Kwakiutl Indians, along with the Tsimshian, Haida, Bella Coola, Nootka, and some of the Coast Salish came under the jurisdiction of the Canadian government. Government officials disapproved of how much property was destroyed at potlatches. Furthermore, Christian missionaries complained to them that the potlatches were the greatest obstacle they faced in making the Indians convert to Christianity.

In 1884, the Canadian government made it a criminal offense to hold potlatches and the Winter Ceremonies. Anyone caught disobeying could go to jail. While the activities were sometimes continued in secrecy, they greatly declined.

Meanwhile, in the United States and Canada, village sites of local groups became designated as reservations, and children were sent to mission schools, where they were made charges of various Christian churches. In the schools, the children were not allowed to speak in their native tongue, nor to draw in their traditional way. They got out of school and found themselves unsure about their own identities. As they struggled to figure out where they belonged, the native cultures diminished greatly.

In Alaska, as elsewhere on the Pacific Northwest Coast, life became hard for the natives. In 1867, the United States bought Alaska from Russia. The price of $7.2 million was a big bargain (about 2 cents per acre), but many Americans thought the purchase was a waste of money, and they called it Seward's Folly, after U.S. Secretary of State William H. Seward, who had arranged the purchase.

American ships began to visit New Archangel, now known as Sitka, and to trade with Indian villages. American hunting soon made seals as rare as the sea otter. The Americans also brought new industries to the area. When gold was discovered in Alaska during the 1870s and 1880s, more and more people were attracted to the re-

▶ A Quinault Indian holds a newly caught salmon in Taholah, Washington, the main town on their reservation. This picture was taken in 1936.

▲ Makah Indians camp on a beach near Puget Sound in the 1890s. Their large traveling canoes are drawn up on the sand.

▼ Tulalip Indians in front of their home on the Tulalip Reservation, Washington, in 1916.

▲ A Quinault Indian tries out his new dugout canoe in Taholah in the 1930s. Canoe races are still held here each year.

gion. The newcomers set up salmon canneries and sawmills, both of which intruded on the Indians' way of life.

The thriving fish canneries killed the salmon in far greater quantities than the Indians ever had. And lumberjacks cut down the trees nearest the coast: the same trees the Indians needed, since they could be transported by water.

As the salmon and wood the Indians had relied upon rapidly vanished, the Indians became reduced to poverty. They had nowhere to turn for help, since the United States had as yet developed no policy to deal with Alaska and its people, and the territory was governed without any protection for the Indians.

In order to survive, women now went to work in the canneries and men became lumberjacks. Elsewhere, Indians crafted entire totem pole vil-

lages for sightseers from the other states, who came to observe them from steamboats. The Indians also sold them handwoven baskets, blankets, and carved wooden objects.

Many Indians left the villages they were born in so that they could be closer to the sawmills in which they worked. Other Indians picked up and moved to be nearer to the tourist trade. No longer were people together to share the Winter Ceremonies and the potlatches.

MODERN TRIBAL LIFE

The most important Canadian Indian legislation in the 19th century was the Indian Act of 1876, authorized by the Canadian Parliament. The act recognized the government's responsibility to provide the Indians with adequate health, welfare, and education and to aid in their agricultural and industrial endeavors. It also provided for the control of Indian lands and the money in-

vested by Indian groups in the Indian Trust Fund, set up to protect the money Indians received by selling the natural resources on their property. Until 1951 the act contained the most significant laws governing the Canadian Indians.

However, today all Pacific Northwest Indians, like all others in Canada who are officially registered natives, are governed by the 1951 Indian Act. This act, along with several treaties, grant them special rights concerning education and hunting and fishing on their land.

In 1951, the Canadian government also revoked the law making it a crime to hold the Winter Ceremonies and potlatches. The Indians were no longer subject to fines or imprisonment for practicing their native traditions.

Today, the Native Brotherhood of British Columbia acts as a kind of trade union to protect the interests of Indian commercial fishermen.

Equally noteworthy, a nationwide campaign by Indians had led the Canadian government to refrain from its previous policy of trying to assimilate them. Instead, the government is attempting new ways to transfer the responsibility for running Indian affairs back to the people. However, this policy of self-determination is still in its initial stages.

In the 1970s, there were about 1,400 Haida living on the Queen Charlotte Islands, and about 600 living elsewhere. At the same time, there were over 8,000 Tsimshian throughout British Columbia. The 3,800 Kwakiutl were divided into 16 bands in British Columbia, while the Bella

Coola numbered 600 and lived on a reserve in Bella Coola, also in British Columbia.

Across the border in the United States, the road to the current treatment of American Indians began in 1871 when Congress stopped making treaties with Indian tribes, while it supposedly permitted previous treaties to be honored. Since then, Indian affairs have been regulated by laws. While it is no secret that the United States has broken nearly every treaty it has made with an Indian tribe, many Indian groups now fight within the court system to get their lands back.

Today, the Bureau of Indian Affairs, created by Congress in 1824, is the most important government agency handling Indian matters. Another important federal agency serving Indians is the Indian Health Service, set up in 1955.

In 1978 Congress passed the American Indian Religious Freedom Act to protect the rights of American Indians and Alaska Natives to believe, express, and exercise their traditional religions.

In 1974, a landmark decision of the U.S. Ninth Circuit Court mandated that Indians in Washington State were entitled to 50 percent of the harvestable number of fish destined for tribal use and accustomed fishing grounds. As a result, fishing remains a major economic and cultural resource of the Indian people. In 1980, another law was passed giving Washington State Indians the right to fish in waters that aren't polluted by sewage and chemical wastes. This requires that industries near the waters keep them unpolluted.

Indian tribes in Washington State, as well as in Oregon, have formed organizations to protect their fishing interests. As a result of district laws and organizations, the coastal tribes here today have tribal hatcheries and many progressive commercial fishing practices.

The Quinault, Makah, and Quileute belong to the Northwest Indian Fisheries Commission, representing 19 western Washington tribes. The Quinault continue to live in Washington's Olympic Peninsula, on a heavily forested reservation. They operate a tribal cannery and are active in developing aquaculture—growing seafood in tanks and pens. They also have the last good stand of red cedar on the coast.

According to the 1980 census, in Alaska the term Alaska Native refers to some 64,000 Indians, as well as Inuit and Aleut people who live in

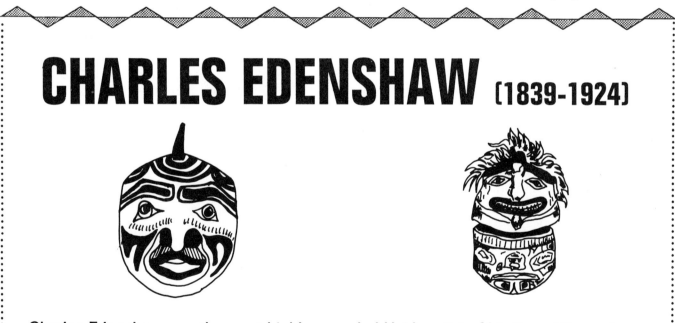

CHARLES EDENSHAW (1839-1924)

Charles Edenshaw was the most highly regarded Haida artist of his time. His work was both traditional and personal. During an illness when he was a teenager, he began carving miniature totem poles out of argillite. Soon his skills increased and he became a master craftsman, carving in both argillite and wood. He was commissioned by many Indians and non-Indians alike. A gifted painter and silversmith as well as a carver, Edenshaw belonged to a high-ranking Haida family.

Alaska. They form 16 percent of Alaska's total population, the highest percentage in any state. Here, the Tlingit and Haida live along the southeastern coast while the Tsimshian live on the Annette Island Reserve in southeastern Alaska.

In Alaska, the Alaskan Native Brotherhood was organized in 1912 to "assist and encourage the native in his advancement . . . " The Tlingit were the main organizers, and the group has Native Sisterhood and Brotherhood Camps in Indian communities. The group campaigns for Indian rights. The Brotherhood's greatest accomplishment may be that for the first time in their history it united the people of all the Indian villages in the region.

In 1971, the U.S. government passed the Alaska Native Claims Settlement Act, giving its natives about one-ninth of Alaskan lands (40 million acres) in exchange for surrendering all claims to any other Alaskan territory. This law divides Alaska into 12 regional native business corporations, each sharing in a payment of around $1 billion.

The shares cannot be sold for a certain number of years, but each person having at least one-quarter Alaskan Native blood owns shares in a village corporation, as well as a regional corporation. This has helped some villages become more self-sufficient.

TRIBAL ARTS REVIVAL

New laws in Canada and the United States have helped to give Northwest Coast Indians more of a voice in their own affairs. Meanwhile, there has also been a revived interest by Indians and non-Indians alike in coastal art. By the 1930s totem poles were on the verge of disappearing, destroyed by weather and vandalism. Then the United States Forest Service began a program to restore the poles. Many poles were removed to protected sites. Others that could be restored were fixed at their original locations.

Since then, Indians have once again begun carving poles and other works of art, both in British Columbia and in the United States. Their work is helping the people recover from the cultural catastrophe they suffered not very long ago. Today, totem pole makers are receiving sizable fees from corporations, museums, and colleges.

Many pieces of Indian art were removed from the region by traders, collectors, and museum curators. It is ironic that the only complete Tsimshian housefront left in the world is found

◄ Haida artist George Gunya carved these beautiful flutes from slate.

▲ A modern version of a Tlingit drum was made in 1971 by Duane Pasco.

in Washington, D.C., at the Smithsonian Institution. The New York Museum of Natural History also has a great deal of Pacific Northwest Coast art. However, in recent years there have been intensive efforts to trace and retrieve many art pieces from around the world.

One of the new native artists is Robert Davidson, the great-grandson of Charles Edenshaw, the Haida's most famous craftsman. Davidson was born in 1946 on the Queen Charlotte Islands. He erected a totem pole in 1969 in the Haida village

of Masset, Queen Charlotte Islands. It was among the first to go up in an Indian village since the start of this century. The new poles are being erected either with government assistance or as gifts from the artists. Raising the poles is always accompanied by much celebration, as in the past. In 1986 he carved three poles that illustrate sto-

▲ On Tillicum Island near Seattle, Native Americans share their heritage with visitors who arrive by boat. The visitors are served a dinner of salmon and then enjoy a performance of traditional dancing and singing. In this picture, the people seated in the background are beating drums made of hollowed logs.

ries about the Killer Whale. These poles have been erected in Purchase, New York, in the PepsiCo sculpture park.

Another important coastal artist of today is Bill Reid, a 70-year-old Haida sculptor, printmaker, and metalsmith. Sixteen of his creations can be found in the Museum of Man in Paris. Bill Reid was once Robert Davidson's teacher. He, too, has carved a totem pole for a Haida village, volunteering his services, although he earns as much as $50,000 for pieces of his gold jewelry.

Modern totem pole makers work by hand with chisels, knives, and adzes that they make themselves. However, they use chainsaws for initial shaping and rough cuts.

Both Davidson and Reid were represented in a recent showing of vivid wooden masks crafted by renowned Northwest Coast native artists in a Vancouver art gallery. Collectors lined up at 4:30 A.M., seven hours before the masks went on sale at prices of up to $12,000. This is evidence of the thriving market for top-quality native art.

But even more important than the prices they earn is the pride these artists are restoring in their people. As the totem poles make a comeback, the heritage of the Pacific Northwest Coast Indians is also returning.

NATIVE AMERICAN LIFE TODAY

THE ARTS

▼ Jesse Cooday and Antonio Rosario used computerized images of Pacific Northwest masks to make this illustration.

PASSING ON TRADITION

◄ Modern Native American artists in the Pacific Northwest continue to create wood carvings using traditional motifs.

▲ Helen Peterson sings a Makah song as Nora Barket beats on a skin drum at a tribal celebration.

◀ Nelson Cross, a modern Haida carver, works with argillite, a black rock brought into prominence by versatile Haida artist Charles Edenshaw.

▶ A modern canoe-maker chips away to produce a cedar dugout at La Push, Washington.

▼ Totem pole carving continues today as an important part of Native American heritage. Here a new pole is carved in Haines, Alaska. A painted house can be seen in the background.

THE FISHING INDUSTRY

▼ · ▼ · ▼ · ▼ · ▼ · ▼ · ▼ · ▼ · ▼

◀ This fish trap in Alaska is called a weir (weer). The fences in the water channel the fish into the boxlike trap. Lawsuits brought by Indians have helped stop many industries from polluting the fishing waters of the Pacific Northwest.

▼ Many Native Americans in the Pacific Northwest continue to fish on their ancestral waters, using traditional methods. However, some are commercial fishermen, using the latest technology.

▲ · ▲ · ▲ · ▲ · ▲ · ▲ · ▲ · ▲ · ▲

INDEX

PICTURE CREDITS